Addition

(With like denominators)

Name

School

CW00848112

DAY : 1

Exercise n°:1 : Multiplication review

$7\times7=$ ...	$9\times5=$ ...	$3\times4=$ ...	$8\times8=$ ...
$4\times3=$ ...	$9\times3=$ ...	$4\times8=$ ...	$9\times5=$ ...

Exercise n°:2 : Adding fractions

Example: $\frac{9}{7}+\frac{2}{7}=\frac{9+2}{7}=\frac{11}{7}$

LCM(7,7) = 7

(1) $\frac{2}{4}+\frac{3}{4}=\frac{\dots\dots+\dots\dots}{\dots\dots}=\frac{\dots\dots}{\dots\dots}$

(2) $\frac{4}{3}+\frac{5}{3}=\frac{\dots\dots+\dots\dots}{\dots\dots}=\frac{\dots\dots}{\dots\dots}$

(3) $\frac{8}{9}+\frac{9}{9}=\frac{\dots\dots+\dots\dots}{\dots\dots}=\frac{\dots\dots}{\dots\dots}$

(4) $\frac{5}{6}+\frac{4}{6}=\frac{\dots\dots+\dots\dots}{\dots\dots}=\frac{\dots\dots}{\dots\dots}$

(5) $3+\frac{1}{8}=\frac{\dots\dots+\dots\dots}{\dots\dots}=\frac{\dots\dots}{\dots\dots}$

(6) $\frac{4}{9}+\frac{5}{9}=\frac{\dots\dots+\dots\dots}{\dots\dots}=\frac{\dots\dots}{\dots\dots}$

Answer key	Score
(1) $\frac{5}{4}$ (2) $\frac{9}{3}$ (3) $\frac{17}{9}$ (4) $\frac{9}{6}$ (5) $\frac{25}{8}$ (6) $\frac{9}{9}$	/6

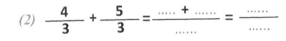

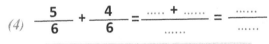

LCM= Least Common Multiple

Addition

(With like denominators)

Name: ....

School: ....

DAY: 2

Exercise n°:1 : Multiplication review

$1\times1=$ ...	$2\times5=$ ...	$6\times4=$ ...	$4\times4=$ ...
$1\times6=$ ...	$4\times6=$ ...	$1\times3=$ ...	$5\times9=$ ...

Exercise n°:2 : Adding fractions

Example: $\frac{6}{1}+\frac{8}{1}=\frac{6+8}{1}=\frac{14}{1}$

LCM(1,1) = 1

(1) $\frac{4}{4}+\frac{8}{4}=\frac{\dots+\dots}{\dots}=\frac{\dots}{\dots}$

(2) $\frac{1}{6}+\frac{5}{6}=\frac{\dots+\dots}{\dots}=\frac{\dots}{\dots}$

(3) $\frac{3}{5}+\frac{2}{5}=\frac{\dots+\dots}{\dots}=\frac{\dots}{\dots}$

(4) $\frac{9}{7}+\frac{8}{7}=\frac{\dots+\dots}{\dots}=\frac{\dots}{\dots}$

(5) $2+\frac{8}{4}=\frac{\dots+\dots}{\dots}=\frac{\dots}{\dots}$

(6) $\frac{9}{2}+\frac{6}{2}=\frac{\dots+\dots}{\dots}=\frac{\dots}{\dots}$

Answer key	Score
(1) $\frac{12}{4}$ (2) $\frac{6}{6}$ (3) $\frac{5}{5}$ (4) $\frac{17}{7}$ (5) $\frac{16}{4}$ (6) $\frac{15}{2}$	/6

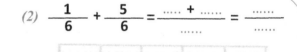

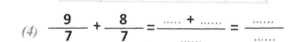

LCM= *Least Common Multiple*

Addition

(With unlike denominators)

Name: ....

School: ....

DAY: 3

Exercise n°:1 : Multiplication review

$7\times9=$ ... $7\times5=$ ... $4\times8=$ ... $8\times8=$ ...

$6\times4=$ ... $8\times1=$ ... $6\times5=$ ... $1\times1=$ ...

Exercise n°:2 : Adding fractions

Example: $\frac{4}{7}+\frac{9}{9}=\frac{36+63}{63}=\frac{99}{63}$

LCM(7,9) = 63

(1) $\frac{8}{6}+\frac{6}{4}=\frac{\dots + \dots}{\dots}=\frac{\dots}{\dots}$

(2) $\frac{6}{4}+\frac{5}{1}=\frac{\dots + \dots}{\dots}=\frac{\dots}{\dots}$

(3) $\frac{5}{1}+\frac{1}{1}=\frac{\dots + \dots}{\dots}=\frac{\dots}{\dots}$

(4) $\frac{1}{2}+\frac{3}{8}=\frac{\dots + \dots}{\dots}=\frac{\dots}{\dots}$

(5) $4+\frac{8}{8}=\frac{\dots + \dots}{\dots}=\frac{\dots}{\dots}$

(6) $\frac{9}{3}+\frac{7}{7}=\frac{\dots + \dots}{\dots}=\frac{\dots}{\dots}$

Answer key	Score
(1) $\frac{34}{12}$ (2) $\frac{26}{4}$ (3) $\frac{6}{1}$ (4) $\frac{7}{8}$ (5) $\frac{40}{8}$ (6) $\frac{84}{21}$	/6

LCM= **L**east **C**ommon **M**ultiple

Addition

(With unlike denominators)

Name: ....

School: ....

DAY: 4

Exercise n°:1 : Multiplication review

$3\times5=$ ... $\quad 5\times5=$ ... $\quad 8\times9=$ ... $\quad 6\times6=$ ...

$8\times8=$ ... $\quad 9\times7=$ ... $\quad 8\times9=$ ... $\quad 5\times5=$ ...

Exercise n°:2 : Adding fractions

Example: $\frac{1}{3}+\frac{2}{5}=\frac{5+6}{15}=\frac{11}{15}$

LCM(3,5) = 15

(1) $\frac{5}{1}+\frac{1}{2}=\frac{\dots+\dots}{\dots}=\frac{\dots}{\dots}$

(2) $\frac{8}{8}+\frac{5}{7}=\frac{\dots+\dots}{\dots}=\frac{\dots}{\dots}$

(3) $\frac{9}{5}+\frac{1}{9}=\frac{\dots+\dots}{\dots}=\frac{\dots}{\dots}$

(4) $\frac{5}{7}+\frac{3}{8}=\frac{\dots+\dots}{\dots}=\frac{\dots}{\dots}$

(5) $5+\frac{2}{6}=\frac{\dots+\dots}{\dots}=\frac{\dots}{\dots}$

(6) $\frac{6}{4}+\frac{6}{5}=\frac{\dots+\dots}{\dots}=\frac{\dots}{\dots}$

Answer key	Score
(1) $\frac{11}{2}$ (2) $\frac{96}{56}$ (3) $\frac{86}{45}$ (4) $\frac{61}{56}$ (5) $\frac{32}{9}$ (6) $\frac{54}{20}$	/6

LCM= Least Common Multiple

Addition

(With unlike denominators)

Name: ....

School: ....

DAY: 5

Exercise n°:1 : Multiplication review

$9\times3 =$ ... $3\times6 =$ ... $2\times9 =$ ... $7\times7 =$ ...

$8\times2 =$ ... $4\times2=$ ... $8\times8=$ ... $4\times4 =$ ...

Exercise n°:2 : Adding fractions

Example: $\frac{7}{9} + \frac{7}{3} = \frac{7 + 21}{9} = \frac{28}{9}$

LCM(9,3) = 9

(1) $\frac{4}{7} + \frac{9}{9} = \frac{\dots + \dots}{\dots} = \frac{\dots}{\dots}$

(2) $\frac{8}{2} + \frac{6}{2} = \frac{\dots + \dots}{\dots} = \frac{\dots}{\dots}$

(3) $\frac{8}{4} + \frac{2}{4} = \frac{\dots + \dots}{\dots} = \frac{\dots}{\dots}$

(4) $\frac{4}{7} + \frac{5}{6} = \frac{\dots + \dots}{\dots} = \frac{\dots}{\dots}$

(5) $2 + \frac{6}{7} = \frac{\dots + \dots}{\dots} = \frac{\dots}{\dots}$

(6) $\frac{4}{8} + \frac{7}{3} = \frac{\dots + \dots}{\dots} = \frac{\dots}{\dots}$

Answer key	Score
(1) $\frac{99}{63}$ (2) $\frac{14}{2}$ (3) $\frac{10}{4}$ (4) $\frac{59}{42}$ (5) $\frac{20}{7}$ (6) $\frac{68}{24}$	/6

LCM= **L**east **C**ommon **M**ultiple

Addition

(With unlike denominators)

Name: ....

School: ....

DAY: 6

Exercise n°:1 : Multiplication review

$6\times8=$ ...	$9\times9=$ ...	$2\times1=$ ...	$2\times2=$ ...
$7\times2=$ ...	$6\times3=$ ...	$7\times7=$ ...	$1\times4=$ ...

Exercise n°:2 : Adding fractions

Example: $\frac{5}{6}+\frac{4}{8}=\frac{20+12}{24}=\frac{32}{24}$

LCM(6,8) = 24

(1) $\frac{3}{9}+\frac{4}{2}=\frac{\ldots+\ldots}{\ldots}=\frac{\ldots}{\ldots}$

(2) $\frac{7}{2}+\frac{9}{3}=\frac{\ldots+\ldots}{\ldots}=\frac{\ldots}{\ldots}$

(3) $\frac{7}{1}+\frac{3}{1}=\frac{\ldots+\ldots}{\ldots}=\frac{\ldots}{\ldots}$

(4) $\frac{4}{6}+\frac{6}{6}=\frac{\ldots+\ldots}{\ldots}=\frac{\ldots}{\ldots}$

(5) $9+\frac{7}{2}=\frac{\ldots+\ldots}{\ldots}=\frac{\ldots}{\ldots}$

(6) $\frac{3}{7}+\frac{2}{9}=\frac{\ldots+\ldots}{\ldots}=\frac{\ldots}{\ldots}$

Answer key	Score
(1) $\frac{42}{18}$ (2) $\frac{39}{6}$ (3) $\frac{10}{1}$ (4) $\frac{10}{6}$ (5) $\frac{25}{2}$ (6) $\frac{41}{63}$	/6

*LCM= **L**east **C**ommon **M**ultiple*

Addition

(With unlike denominators)

Name: ....

School: ....

DAY: 7

Exercise n°:1 : Multiplication review

$8\times1 =$ ...	$9\times2 =$ ...	$8\times9 =$ ...	$1\times1 =$ ...
$7\times8 =$ ...	$1\times5=$ ...	$7\times5=$ ...	$3\times7 =$ ...

Exercise n°:2 : Adding fractions

Example: $\frac{9}{8}+\frac{8}{1}=\frac{9\ +\ 64}{8}=\frac{73}{8}$

LCM(8,1) = 8

(1) $\frac{6}{8}+\frac{8}{3}=\frac{\dots + \dots}{\dots}=\frac{\dots}{\dots}$

(2) $\frac{7}{8}+\frac{2}{5}=\frac{\dots + \dots}{\dots}=\frac{\dots}{\dots}$

(3) $\frac{5}{3}+\frac{9}{2}=\frac{\dots + \dots}{\dots}=\frac{\dots}{\dots}$

(4) $\frac{7}{6}+\frac{7}{8}=\frac{\dots + \dots}{\dots}=\frac{\dots}{\dots}$

(5) $5+\frac{5}{1}=\frac{\dots + \dots}{\dots}=\frac{\dots}{\dots}$

(6) $\frac{1}{3}+\frac{2}{9}=\frac{\dots + \dots}{\dots}=\frac{\dots}{\dots}$

Answer key	Score
(1) $\frac{82}{24}$ (2) $\frac{51}{40}$ (3) $\frac{37}{6}$ (4) $\frac{49}{24}$ (5) $\frac{10}{1}$ (6) $\frac{5}{9}$	/6

LCM= Least Common Multiple

Addition

(With unlike denominators)

Name: ....

School: ....

DAY: 8

Exercise n°:1 : Multiplication review

$9 \times 1 = \ldots$	$3 \times 8 = \ldots$	$9 \times 7 = \ldots$	$8 \times 8 = \ldots$
$4 \times 9 = \ldots$	$6 \times 6 = \ldots$	$4 \times 7 = \ldots$	$8 \times 6 = \ldots$

Exercise n°:2 : Adding fractions

Example: $\frac{2}{9} + \frac{6}{1} = \frac{2 + 54}{9} = \frac{56}{9}$

LCM(9,1) = 9

(1) $\frac{7}{5} + \frac{9}{3} = \frac{\ldots + \ldots}{\ldots} = \frac{\ldots}{\ldots}$

(2) $\frac{4}{9} + \frac{8}{6} = \frac{\ldots + \ldots}{\ldots} = \frac{\ldots}{\ldots}$

(3) $\frac{7}{8} + \frac{4}{3} = \frac{\ldots + \ldots}{\ldots} = \frac{\ldots}{\ldots}$

(4) $\frac{6}{5} + \frac{9}{1} = \frac{\ldots + \ldots}{\ldots} = \frac{\ldots}{\ldots}$

(5) $5 + \frac{9}{8} = \frac{\ldots + \ldots}{\ldots} = \frac{\ldots}{\ldots}$

(6) $\frac{6}{4} + \frac{1}{3} = \frac{\ldots + \ldots}{\ldots} = \frac{\ldots}{\ldots}$

Answer key	Score
(1) $\frac{66}{15}$ (2) $\frac{32}{18}$ (3) $\frac{53}{24}$ (4) $\frac{51}{5}$ (5) $\frac{49}{8}$ (6) $\frac{22}{12}$	/6

*LCM= **L**east **C**ommon **M**ultiple*

Addition

(With unlike denominators)

Name: ....

School: ....

DAY: 9

Exercise n°:1 : Multiplication review

$9\times2=$ ...	$7\times4=$ ...	$3\times3=$ ...	$8\times8=$ ...
$8\times3=$ ...	$7\times6=$ ...	$8\times1=$ ...	$8\times1=$ ...

Exercise n°:2 : Adding fractions

Example: $\frac{2}{9}+\frac{2}{2}=\frac{4+18}{18}=\frac{22}{18}$

LCM(9,2) = 18

(1) $\frac{9}{2}+\frac{7}{4}=\frac{\ldots+\ldots}{\ldots}=\frac{\ldots}{\ldots}$

(2) $\frac{8}{3}+\frac{4}{6}=\frac{\ldots+\ldots}{\ldots}=\frac{\ldots}{\ldots}$

(3) $\frac{1}{8}+\frac{4}{8}=\frac{\ldots+\ldots}{\ldots}=\frac{\ldots}{\ldots}$

(4) $\frac{1}{5}+\frac{6}{9}=\frac{\ldots+\ldots}{\ldots}=\frac{\ldots}{\ldots}$

(5) $7+\frac{8}{8}=\frac{\ldots+\ldots}{\ldots}=\frac{\ldots}{\ldots}$

(6) $\frac{2}{2}+\frac{5}{7}=\frac{\ldots+\ldots}{\ldots}=\frac{\ldots}{\ldots}$

Answer key	Score
(1) $\frac{25}{4}$ (2) $\frac{20}{6}$ (3) $\frac{5}{8}$ (4) $\frac{39}{45}$ (5) $\frac{64}{8}$ (6) $\frac{24}{14}$	/6

*LCM= **L**east **C**ommon **M**ultiple*

Addition

(With unlike denominators)

Name: ....

School: ....

DAY: 10

Exercise n°:1 : Multiplication review

$1\times3=$ ...	$4\times4=$ ...	$4\times6=$ ...	$9\times9=$ ...
$3\times4=$ ...	$8\times3=$ ...	$3\times9=$ ...	$6\times4=$ ...

Exercise n°:2 : Adding fractions

Example: $\frac{5}{1}+\frac{1}{3}=\frac{15+1}{3}=\frac{16}{3}$

LCM(1,3) = 3

(1) $\frac{2}{3}+\frac{2}{7}=\frac{\dots+\dots}{\dots}=\frac{\dots}{\dots}$

(2) $\frac{3}{4}+\frac{4}{3}=\frac{\dots+\dots}{\dots}=\frac{\dots}{\dots}$

(3) $\frac{9}{6}+\frac{6}{2}=\frac{\dots+\dots}{\dots}=\frac{\dots}{\dots}$

(4) $\frac{4}{3}+\frac{3}{7}=\frac{\dots+\dots}{\dots}=\frac{\dots}{\dots}$

(5) $3+\frac{2}{9}=\frac{\dots+\dots}{\dots}=\frac{\dots}{\dots}$

(6) $\frac{4}{8}+\frac{7}{4}=\frac{\dots+\dots}{\dots}=\frac{\dots}{\dots}$

Answer key	Score
(1) $\frac{20}{21}$ (2) $\frac{25}{12}$ (3) $\frac{27}{6}$ (4) $\frac{37}{21}$ (5) $\frac{29}{9}$ (6) $\frac{18}{8}$	/6

LCM= Least Common Multiple

Addition

(With unlike denominators)

Name: ....

School: ....

DAY: 11

Exercise n°:1 : Multiplication review

$5\times5=$ ...	$8\times5=$ ...	$1\times2=$ ...	$4\times4=$ ...
$2\times1=$ ...	$1\times5=$ ...	$2\times3=$ ...	$5\times9=$ ...

Exercise n°:2 : Adding fractions

Example: $\frac{1}{5}+\frac{5}{5}=\frac{1+5}{5}=\frac{6}{5}$

LCM(5,5) = 5

(1) $\frac{7}{8}+\frac{4}{8}=\frac{\dots+\dots}{\dots}=\frac{\dots}{\dots}$

(2) $\frac{2}{1}+\frac{5}{5}=\frac{\dots+\dots}{\dots}=\frac{\dots}{\dots}$

(3) $\frac{3}{5}+\frac{1}{7}=\frac{\dots+\dots}{\dots}=\frac{\dots}{\dots}$

(4) $\frac{9}{9}+\frac{2}{7}=\frac{\dots+\dots}{\dots}=\frac{\dots}{\dots}$

(5) $4+\frac{6}{4}=\frac{\dots+\dots}{\dots}=\frac{\dots}{\dots}$

(6) $\frac{3}{4}+\frac{2}{8}=\frac{\dots+\dots}{\dots}=\frac{\dots}{\dots}$

Answer key	Score
(1) $\frac{11}{8}$ (2) $\frac{15}{5}$ (3) $\frac{26}{35}$ (4) $\frac{81}{63}$ (5) $\frac{22}{4}$ (6) $\frac{8}{8}$	/6

*LCM= **L**east **C**ommon **M**ultiple*

Addition

(With unlike denominators)

Name: ....

School: ....

DAY: 12

Exercise n°:1 : Multiplication review

$1\times3 = ...$	$7\times5 = ...$	$6\times3 = ...$	$5\times5 = ...$
$6\times6 = ...$	$3\times2= ...$	$6\times5= ...$	$5\times1 = ...$

Exercise n°:2 : Adding fractions

Example: $\frac{5}{1} + \frac{2}{3} = \frac{15 + 2}{3} = \frac{17}{3}$

LCM(1,3) = 3

(1) $\frac{3}{9} + \frac{5}{7} = \frac{..... + ...}{......} = \frac{......}{......}$

(2) $\frac{6}{6} + \frac{5}{2} = \frac{..... + ...}{......} = \frac{......}{......}$

(3) $\frac{5}{5} + \frac{1}{2} = \frac{..... + ...}{......} = \frac{......}{......}$

(4) $\frac{1}{8} + \frac{3}{6} = \frac{..... + ...}{......} = \frac{......}{......}$

(5) $5 + \frac{1}{5} = \frac{..... + ...}{......} = \frac{......}{......}$

(6) $\frac{4}{9} + \frac{3}{7} = \frac{..... + ...}{......} = \frac{......}{......}$

Answer key	Score
(1) $\frac{66}{63}$ (2) $\frac{21}{6}$ (3) $\frac{15}{10}$ (4) $\frac{15}{24}$ (5) $\frac{26}{5}$ (6) $\frac{55}{63}$	/6

*LCM= **L**east **C**ommon **M**ultiple*

Addition

(With unlike denominators)

Name: ....

School: ....

DAY: 13

Exercise n°:1 : Multiplication review

$5\times1=$ ...	$4\times1=$ ...	$6\times9=$ ...	$3\times3=$ ...
$7\times6=$ ...	$5\times3=$ ...	$7\times5=$ ...	$9\times6=$ ...

Exercise n°:2 : Adding fractions

Example: $\frac{4}{5}+\frac{1}{1}=\frac{4+5}{5}=\frac{9}{5}$

LCM(5,1) = 5

(1) $\frac{4}{7}+\frac{7}{7}=\frac{\dots+\dots}{\dots}=\frac{\dots}{\dots}$

(2) $\frac{7}{6}+\frac{1}{3}=\frac{\dots+\dots}{\dots}=\frac{\dots}{\dots}$

(3) $\frac{5}{9}+\frac{6}{1}=\frac{\dots+\dots}{\dots}=\frac{\dots}{\dots}$

(4) $\frac{6}{3}+\frac{9}{3}=\frac{\dots+\dots}{\dots}=\frac{\dots}{\dots}$

(5) $9+\frac{6}{3}=\frac{\dots+\dots}{\dots}=\frac{\dots}{\dots}$

(6) $\frac{9}{9}+\frac{7}{4}=\frac{\dots+\dots}{\dots}=\frac{\dots}{\dots}$

Answer key	Score
(1) $\frac{11}{7}$ (2) $\frac{9}{6}$ (3) $\frac{59}{9}$ (4) $\frac{15}{3}$ (5) $\frac{33}{3}$ (6) $\frac{99}{36}$	/6

LCM= **L**east **C**ommon **M**ultiple

Addition

(With unlike denominators)

Name: ....

School: ....

DAY: 14

Exercise n°:1 : Multiplication review

$4\times5=$ ...	$8\times1=$ ...	$1\times9=$ ...	$8\times8=$ ...
$8\times1=$ ...	$9\times5=$ ...	$8\times6=$ ...	$4\times3=$ ...

Exercise n°:2 : Adding fractions

Example: $\frac{6}{4}+\frac{8}{5}=\frac{30+32}{20}=\frac{62}{20}$

LCM(4,5) = 20

(1) $\frac{3}{8}+\frac{9}{5}=\frac{\dots\dots+\dots\dots}{\dots\dots}=\frac{\dots\dots}{\dots\dots}$

(2) $\frac{8}{1}+\frac{1}{5}=\frac{\dots\dots+\dots\dots}{\dots\dots}=\frac{\dots\dots}{\dots\dots}$

(3) $\frac{6}{4}+\frac{1}{7}=\frac{\dots\dots+\dots\dots}{\dots\dots}=\frac{\dots\dots}{\dots\dots}$

(4) $\frac{3}{8}+\frac{7}{6}=\frac{\dots\dots+\dots\dots}{\dots\dots}=\frac{\dots\dots}{\dots\dots}$

(5) $7+\frac{9}{8}=\frac{\dots\dots+\dots\dots}{\dots\dots}=\frac{\dots\dots}{\dots\dots}$

(6) $\frac{4}{6}+\frac{4}{8}=\frac{\dots\dots+\dots\dots}{\dots\dots}=\frac{\dots\dots}{\dots\dots}$

Answer key	Score
(1) $\frac{87}{40}$ (2) $\frac{41}{5}$ (3) $\frac{46}{28}$ (4) $\frac{37}{24}$ (5) $\frac{65}{8}$ (6) $\frac{28}{24}$	/6

LCM= **L**east **C**ommon **M**ultiple

Addition

(With unlike denominators)

Name: ....

School: ....

DAY: 15

Exercise n°:1 : Multiplication review

$6\times 9 = ...$	$9\times 1 = ...$	$8\times 5 = ...$	$9\times 9 = ...$
$2\times 8 = ...$	$1\times 2 = ...$	$2\times 9 = ...$	$6\times 8 = ...$

Exercise n°:2 : Adding fractions

Example: $\frac{1}{6} + \frac{7}{9} = \frac{3 + 14}{18} = \frac{17}{18}$

LCM(6,9) = 18

(1) $\frac{6}{4} + \frac{9}{9} = \frac{..... + ...}{.....} = \frac{.....}{.....}$

(2) $\frac{2}{8} + \frac{1}{2} = \frac{..... + ...}{.....} = \frac{.....}{.....}$

(3) $\frac{9}{6} + \frac{1}{6} = \frac{..... + ...}{.....} = \frac{.....}{.....}$

(4) $\frac{8}{6} + \frac{6}{3} = \frac{..... + ...}{.....} = \frac{.....}{.....}$

(5) $8 + \frac{6}{9} = \frac{..... + ...}{.....} = \frac{.....}{.....}$

(6) $\frac{1}{3} + \frac{3}{9} = \frac{..... + ...}{.....} = \frac{.....}{.....}$

Answer key	Score
(1) $\frac{90}{36}$ (2) $\frac{6}{8}$ (3) $\frac{10}{6}$ (4) $\frac{20}{6}$ (5) $\frac{78}{9}$ (6) $\frac{6}{9}$	/6

*LCM= **L**east **C**ommon **M**ultiple*

Addition

(With unlike denominators)

Name: ....

School: ....

DAY: 16

Exercise n°:1 : Multiplication review

$6\times2=$ ...	$8\times9=$ ...	$5\times5=$ ...	$1\times1=$ ...
$6\times5=$ ...	$3\times3=$ ...	$6\times3=$ ...	$3\times2=$ ...

Exercise n°:2 : Adding fractions

Example: $\frac{9}{6}+\frac{7}{2}=\frac{9+21}{6}=\frac{30}{6}$

LCM(6,2) = 6

(1) $\frac{1}{2}+\frac{8}{3}=\frac{\dots+\dots}{\dots}=\frac{\dots}{\dots}$

(2) $\frac{6}{5}+\frac{9}{3}=\frac{\dots+\dots}{\dots}=\frac{\dots}{\dots}$

(3) $\frac{3}{3}+\frac{8}{1}=\frac{\dots+\dots}{\dots}=\frac{\dots}{\dots}$

(4) $\frac{2}{2}+\frac{6}{1}=\frac{\dots+\dots}{\dots}=\frac{\dots}{\dots}$

(5) $2+\frac{2}{1}=\frac{\dots+\dots}{\dots}=\frac{\dots}{\dots}$

(6) $\frac{8}{8}+\frac{9}{8}=\frac{\dots+\dots}{\dots}=\frac{\dots}{\dots}$

Answer key	Score
(1) $\frac{19}{6}$ (2) $\frac{63}{15}$ (3) $\frac{27}{3}$ (4) $\frac{14}{2}$ (5) $\frac{4}{1}$ (6) $\frac{17}{8}$	/6

*LCM= **L**east **C**ommon **M**ultiple*

Addition

(With unlike denominators)

Name: ....

School: ....

DAY: 17

Exercise n°:1 : Multiplication review

$3\times8=$ ...	$4\times4=$ ...	$6\times3=$ ...	$9\times9=$ ...
$3\times6=$ ...	$1\times7=$ ...	$3\times8=$ ...	$4\times6=$ ...

Exercise n°:2 : Adding fractions

Example: $\frac{2}{3}+\frac{6}{8}=\frac{16\ +\ 18}{24}=\frac{34}{24}$

LCM(3,8) = 24

(1) $\frac{7}{5}+\frac{7}{5}=\frac{\ldots\ +\ \ldots}{\ldots}=\frac{\ldots}{\ldots}$

(2) $\frac{3}{6}+\frac{4}{7}=\frac{\ldots\ +\ \ldots}{\ldots}=\frac{\ldots}{\ldots}$

(3) $\frac{8}{4}+\frac{8}{4}=\frac{\ldots\ +\ \ldots}{\ldots}=\frac{\ldots}{\ldots}$

(4) $\frac{6}{6}+\frac{3}{8}=\frac{\ldots\ +\ \ldots}{\ldots}=\frac{\ldots}{\ldots}$

(5) $5+\frac{1}{9}=\frac{\ldots\ +\ \ldots}{\ldots}=\frac{\ldots}{\ldots}$

(6) $\frac{9}{6}+\frac{5}{4}=\frac{\ldots\ +\ \ldots}{\ldots}=\frac{\ldots}{\ldots}$

Answer key	Score
(1) $\frac{14}{5}$ (2) $\frac{45}{42}$ (3) $\frac{16}{4}$ (4) $\frac{33}{24}$ (5) $\frac{46}{9}$ (6) $\frac{33}{12}$	/6

LCM= **L**east **C**ommon **M**ultiple

Addition

(With unlike denominators)

Name: ....

School: ....

DAY: 18

Exercise n°:1 : Multiplication review

$2 \times 7 = \ldots$	$8 \times 7 = \ldots$	$9 \times 5 = \ldots$	$6 \times 6 = \ldots$
$8 \times 9 = \ldots$	$7 \times 6 = \ldots$	$8 \times 7 = \ldots$	$9 \times 1 = \ldots$

Exercise n°:2 : Adding fractions

Example: $\frac{1}{2} + \frac{8}{7} = \frac{7 + 16}{14} = \frac{23}{14}$

LCM(2,7) = 14

(1) $\frac{9}{5} + \frac{5}{3} = \frac{\ldots + \ldots}{\ldots} = \frac{\ldots}{\ldots}$

(2) $\frac{8}{9} + \frac{7}{6} = \frac{\ldots + \ldots}{\ldots} = \frac{\ldots}{\ldots}$

(3) $\frac{7}{9} + \frac{2}{9} = \frac{\ldots + \ldots}{\ldots} = \frac{\ldots}{\ldots}$

(4) $\frac{1}{2} + \frac{9}{7} = \frac{\ldots + \ldots}{\ldots} = \frac{\ldots}{\ldots}$

(5) $6 + \frac{4}{6} = \frac{\ldots + \ldots}{\ldots} = \frac{\ldots}{\ldots}$

(6) $\frac{9}{1} + \frac{6}{8} = \frac{\ldots + \ldots}{\ldots} = \frac{\ldots}{\ldots}$

Answer key	Score
(1) $\frac{52}{15}$ (2) $\frac{37}{18}$ (3) $\frac{9}{9}$ (4) $\frac{25}{14}$ (5) $\frac{40}{6}$ (6) $\frac{78}{8}$	/6

LCM= **L**east **C**ommon **M**ultiple

Addition

(With unlike denominators)

Name: ....

School: ....

DAY: 19

Exercise n°:1 : Multiplication review

$1\times6=$ ... $\quad 9\times6=$ ... $\quad 7\times4=$ ... $\quad 3\times3=$ ...

$5\times7=$ ... $\quad 7\times5=$ ... $\quad 5\times9=$ ... $\quad 4\times2=$ ...

Exercise n°:2 : Adding fractions

Example: $\frac{3}{1}+\frac{4}{6}=\frac{18+4}{6}=\frac{22}{6}$

LCM(1,6) = 6

(1) $\frac{5}{3}+\frac{8}{3}=\frac{\dots+\dots}{\dots}=\frac{\dots}{\dots}$

(2) $\frac{5}{7}+\frac{6}{5}=\frac{\dots+\dots}{\dots}=\frac{\dots}{\dots}$

(3) $\frac{9}{4}+\frac{8}{5}=\frac{\dots+\dots}{\dots}=\frac{\dots}{\dots}$

(4) $\frac{2}{4}+\frac{3}{1}=\frac{\dots+\dots}{\dots}=\frac{\dots}{\dots}$

(5) $5+\frac{3}{3}=\frac{\dots+\dots}{\dots}=\frac{\dots}{\dots}$

(6) $\frac{7}{8}+\frac{8}{9}=\frac{\dots+\dots}{\dots}=\frac{\dots}{\dots}$

Answer key	Score
(1) $\frac{13}{3}$ (2) $\frac{67}{35}$ (3) $\frac{77}{20}$ (4) $\frac{14}{4}$ (5) $\frac{18}{3}$ (6) $\frac{127}{72}$	/6

LCM= **L**east **C**ommon **M**ultiple

Addition

(With unlike denominators)

Name: ....

School: ....

DAY: 20

Exercise n°:1 : Multiplication review

$2\times2=$ ...	$7\times2=$ ...	$6\times8=$ ...	$8\times8=$ ...
$4\times6=$ ...	$4\times8=$ ...	$4\times6=$ ...	$8\times9=$ ...

Exercise n°:2 : Adding fractions

Example: $\frac{9}{2}+\frac{6}{2}=\frac{9+6}{2}=\frac{15}{2}$

LCM(2,2) = 2

(1) $\frac{2}{3}+\frac{4}{6}=\frac{\dots+\dots}{\dots}=\frac{\dots}{\dots}$

(2) $\frac{4}{6}+\frac{2}{8}=\frac{\dots+\dots}{\dots}=\frac{\dots}{\dots}$

(3) $\frac{6}{8}+\frac{6}{2}=\frac{\dots+\dots}{\dots}=\frac{\dots}{\dots}$

(4) $\frac{9}{4}+\frac{8}{7}=\frac{\dots+\dots}{\dots}=\frac{\dots}{\dots}$

(5) $2+\frac{3}{8}=\frac{\dots+\dots}{\dots}=\frac{\dots}{\dots}$

(6) $\frac{7}{5}+\frac{3}{7}=\frac{\dots+\dots}{\dots}=\frac{\dots}{\dots}$

Answer key	Score
(1) $\frac{8}{6}$ (2) $\frac{22}{24}$ (3) $\frac{30}{8}$ (4) $\frac{95}{28}$ (5) $\frac{19}{8}$ (6) $\frac{64}{35}$	/6

*LCM= **L**east **C**ommon **M**ultiple*

Addition

(With unlike denominators)

Name: ....

School: ....

DAY : 21

Exercise n°:1 : Multiplication review

$5\times8=$ ... $9\times2=$ ... $6\times1=$ ... $8\times8=$ ...

$8\times6=$ ... $6\times1=$ ... $8\times8=$ ... $2\times9=$ ...

Exercise n°:2 : Adding fractions

Example: $\frac{6}{5}+\frac{6}{8}=\frac{48+30}{40}=\frac{78}{40}$

LCM(5,8) = 40

(1) $\frac{8}{8}+\frac{5}{9}=\frac{\dots+\dots}{\dots}=\frac{\dots}{\dots}$

(2) $\frac{8}{6}+\frac{2}{1}=\frac{\dots+\dots}{\dots}=\frac{\dots}{\dots}$

(3) $\frac{8}{2}+\frac{1}{1}=\frac{\dots+\dots}{\dots}=\frac{\dots}{\dots}$

(4) $\frac{9}{2}+\frac{2}{3}=\frac{\dots+\dots}{\dots}=\frac{\dots}{\dots}$

(5) $3+\frac{5}{8}=\frac{\dots+\dots}{\dots}=\frac{\dots}{\dots}$

(6) $\frac{8}{7}+\frac{8}{9}=\frac{\dots+\dots}{\dots}=\frac{\dots}{\dots}$

Answer key	Score
(1) $\frac{112}{72}$ (2) $\frac{20}{6}$ (3) $\frac{10}{2}$ (4) $\frac{31}{6}$ (5) $\frac{29}{8}$ (6) $\frac{128}{63}$	/6

LCM= Least Common Multiple

Addition

(With unlike denominators)

Name: ....

School: ....

DAY: 22

Exercise n°:1 : Multiplication review

$3\times4=$ ...	$6\times9=$ ...	$7\times6=$ ...	$8\times8=$ ...
$8\times7=$ ...	$5\times1=$ ...	$8\times9=$ ...	$4\times6=$ ...

Exercise n°:2 : Adding fractions

Example: $\frac{4}{3}+\frac{1}{4}=\frac{16+3}{12}=\frac{19}{12}$

LCM(3,4) = 12

(1) $\frac{6}{1}+\frac{9}{9}=\frac{\dots\dots+\dots\dots}{\dots\dots}=\frac{\dots\dots}{\dots\dots}$

(2) $\frac{8}{7}+\frac{9}{1}=\frac{\dots\dots+\dots\dots}{\dots\dots}=\frac{\dots\dots}{\dots\dots}$

(3) $\frac{9}{4}+\frac{5}{3}=\frac{\dots\dots+\dots\dots}{\dots\dots}=\frac{\dots\dots}{\dots\dots}$

(4) $\frac{6}{8}+\frac{2}{8}=\frac{\dots\dots+\dots\dots}{\dots\dots}=\frac{\dots\dots}{\dots\dots}$

(5) $2+\frac{3}{8}=\frac{\dots\dots+\dots\dots}{\dots\dots}=\frac{\dots\dots}{\dots\dots}$

(6) $\frac{1}{6}+\frac{5}{6}=\frac{\dots\dots+\dots\dots}{\dots\dots}=\frac{\dots\dots}{\dots\dots}$

Answer key	Score
(1) $\frac{63}{9}$ (2) $\frac{71}{7}$ (3) $\frac{47}{12}$ (4) $\frac{8}{8}$ (5) $\frac{19}{8}$ (6) $\frac{6}{6}$	/6

*LCM= **L**east **C**ommon **M**ultiple*

Addition

Name: ....

School: ....

DAY: 23

(With unlike denominators)

Exercise n°:1 : Multiplication review

$4 \times 1 =$ ...	$1 \times 2 =$ ...	$7 \times 4 =$ ...	$4 \times 4 =$ ...
$9 \times 7 =$ ...	$4 \times 9 =$ ...	$9 \times 6 =$ ...	$9 \times 1 =$ ...

Exercise n°:2 : Adding fractions

Example: $\frac{8}{4} + \frac{5}{1} = \frac{8 + 20}{4} = \frac{28}{4}$

LCM(4,1) = 4

(1) $\frac{3}{9} + \frac{7}{7} = \frac{\ldots + \ldots}{\ldots} = \frac{\ldots}{\ldots}$

(2) $\frac{9}{7} + \frac{2}{9} = \frac{\ldots + \ldots}{\ldots} = \frac{\ldots}{\ldots}$

(3) $\frac{6}{9} + \frac{1}{2} = \frac{\ldots + \ldots}{\ldots} = \frac{\ldots}{\ldots}$

(4) $\frac{1}{5} + \frac{5}{8} = \frac{\ldots + \ldots}{\ldots} = \frac{\ldots}{\ldots}$

(5) $8 + \frac{6}{4} = \frac{\ldots + \ldots}{\ldots} = \frac{\ldots}{\ldots}$

(6) $\frac{1}{2} + \frac{8}{1} = \frac{\ldots + \ldots}{\ldots} = \frac{\ldots}{\ldots}$

Answer key	Score
(1) $\frac{84}{63}$ (2) $\frac{95}{63}$ (3) $\frac{21}{18}$ (4) $\frac{33}{40}$ (5) $\frac{38}{4}$ (6) $\frac{17}{2}$	/6

LCM= **L**east **C**ommon **M**ultiple

Addition

(With unlike denominators)

Name: ....

School: ....

DAY: 24

Exercise n°:1 : Multiplication review

$8 \times 8 = \ldots$ $2 \times 7 = \ldots$ $1 \times 1 = \ldots$ $6 \times 6 = \ldots$

$6 \times 1 = \ldots$ $5 \times 2 = \ldots$ $6 \times 3 = \ldots$ $7 \times 9 = \ldots$

Exercise n°:2 : Adding fractions

Example: $\frac{5}{8} + \frac{4}{8} = \frac{5 + 4}{8} = \frac{9}{8}$

LCM(8,8) = 8

(1) $\frac{9}{5} + \frac{9}{5} = \frac{\ldots + \ldots}{\ldots} = \frac{\ldots}{\ldots}$

(2) $\frac{6}{1} + \frac{7}{2} = \frac{\ldots + \ldots}{\ldots} = \frac{\ldots}{\ldots}$

(3) $\frac{3}{7} + \frac{3}{3} = \frac{\ldots + \ldots}{\ldots} = \frac{\ldots}{\ldots}$

(4) $\frac{9}{2} + \frac{6}{8} = \frac{\ldots + \ldots}{\ldots} = \frac{\ldots}{\ldots}$

(5) $7 + \frac{7}{6} = \frac{\ldots + \ldots}{\ldots} = \frac{\ldots}{\ldots}$

(6) $\frac{8}{1} + \frac{1}{2} = \frac{\ldots + \ldots}{\ldots} = \frac{\ldots}{\ldots}$

Answer key	Score
(1) $\frac{18}{5}$ (2) $\frac{19}{2}$ (3) $\frac{30}{21}$ (4) $\frac{42}{8}$ (5) $\frac{49}{6}$ (6) $\frac{17}{2}$	/6

*LCM= **L**east **C**ommon **M**ultiple*

Addition

(With unlike denominators)

Name: ....

School: ....

DAY: 25

Exercise n°:1 : Multiplication review

$7\times2=\ldots$	$4\times2=\ldots$	$6\times6=\ldots$	$3\times3=\ldots$
$8\times6=\ldots$	$2\times7=\ldots$	$8\times1=\ldots$	$2\times8=\ldots$

Exercise n°:2 : Adding fractions

Example: $\frac{4}{7}+\frac{1}{2}=\frac{8+7}{14}=\frac{15}{14}$

LCM(7,2) = 14

(1) $\frac{6}{9}+\frac{4}{6}=\frac{\ldots+\ldots}{\ldots}=\frac{\ldots}{\ldots}$

(2) $\frac{8}{6}+\frac{2}{7}=\frac{\ldots+\ldots}{\ldots}=\frac{\ldots}{\ldots}$

(3) $\frac{1}{2}+\frac{2}{6}=\frac{\ldots+\ldots}{\ldots}=\frac{\ldots}{\ldots}$

(4) $\frac{8}{1}+\frac{5}{4}=\frac{\ldots+\ldots}{\ldots}=\frac{\ldots}{\ldots}$

(5) $7+\frac{9}{3}=\frac{\ldots+\ldots}{\ldots}=\frac{\ldots}{\ldots}$

(6) $\frac{4}{6}+\frac{5}{4}=\frac{\ldots+\ldots}{\ldots}=\frac{\ldots}{\ldots}$

Answer key	Score
(1) $\frac{24}{18}$ (2) $\frac{68}{42}$ (3) $\frac{5}{6}$ (4) $\frac{37}{4}$ (5) $\frac{30}{3}$ (6) $\frac{23}{12}$	/6

*LCM= **L**east **C**ommon **M**ultiple*

Addition

(With unlike denominators)

Name: ....

School: ....

DAY: 26

Exercise n°:1 : Multiplication review

$6\times 2 = \ldots$	$8\times 1 = \ldots$	$5\times 9 = \ldots$	$7\times 7 = \ldots$
$1\times 5 = \ldots$	$3\times 2 = \ldots$	$1\times 3 = \ldots$	$7\times 4 = \ldots$

Exercise n°:2 : Adding fractions

Example: $\frac{1}{6} + \frac{9}{2} = \frac{1 + 27}{6} = \frac{28}{6}$

LCM(6,2) = 6

(1) $\frac{8}{9} + \frac{9}{1} = \frac{\ldots + \ldots}{\ldots} = \frac{\ldots}{\ldots}$

(2) $\frac{1}{5} + \frac{1}{2} = \frac{\ldots + \ldots}{\ldots} = \frac{\ldots}{\ldots}$

(3) $\frac{3}{7} + \frac{6}{4} = \frac{\ldots + \ldots}{\ldots} = \frac{\ldots}{\ldots}$

(4) $\frac{4}{5} + \frac{6}{2} = \frac{\ldots + \ldots}{\ldots} = \frac{\ldots}{\ldots}$

(5) $6 + \frac{8}{7} = \frac{\ldots + \ldots}{\ldots} = \frac{\ldots}{\ldots}$

(6) $\frac{3}{2} + \frac{9}{8} = \frac{\ldots + \ldots}{\ldots} = \frac{\ldots}{\ldots}$

Answer key	Score
(1) $\frac{89}{9}$ (2) $\frac{7}{10}$ (3) $\frac{54}{28}$ (4) $\frac{38}{10}$ (5) $\frac{50}{7}$ (6) $\frac{21}{8}$	/6

*LCM= **L**east **C**ommon **M**ultiple*

Addition

Name: ....

School: ....

DAY: 27

(With unlike denominators)

Exercise n°:1 : Multiplication review

$2\times 2 = \ldots$	$2\times 9 = \ldots$	$2\times 5 = \ldots$	$5\times 5 = \ldots$
$9\times 2 = \ldots$	$1\times 3 = \ldots$	$9\times 5 = \ldots$	$6\times 3 = \ldots$

Exercise n°:2 : Adding fractions

Example: $\frac{8}{2} + \frac{9}{2} = \frac{8+9}{2} = \frac{17}{2}$

LCM(2,2) = 2

(1) $\frac{2}{4} + \frac{5}{3} = \frac{\ldots + \ldots}{\ldots} = \frac{\ldots}{\ldots}$

(2) $\frac{9}{2} + \frac{9}{3} = \frac{\ldots + \ldots}{\ldots} = \frac{\ldots}{\ldots}$

(3) $\frac{5}{6} + \frac{6}{7} = \frac{\ldots + \ldots}{\ldots} = \frac{\ldots}{\ldots}$

(4) $\frac{3}{7} + \frac{3}{9} = \frac{\ldots + \ldots}{\ldots} = \frac{\ldots}{\ldots}$

(5) $9 + \frac{4}{5} = \frac{\ldots + \ldots}{\ldots} = \frac{\ldots}{\ldots}$

(6) $\frac{9}{1} + \frac{9}{2} = \frac{\ldots + \ldots}{\ldots} = \frac{\ldots}{\ldots}$

Answer key	Score
(1) $\frac{26}{12}$ (2) $\frac{45}{6}$ (3) $\frac{71}{42}$ (4) $\frac{48}{63}$ (5) $\frac{49}{5}$ (6) $\frac{27}{2}$	/6

*LCM= **L**east **C**ommon **M**ultiple*

Addition

(With unlike denominators)

Name: ....

School: ....

DAY : 28

Exercise n°:1 : Multiplication review

$8\times2=$ ...	$4\times4=$ ...	$1\times9=$ ...	$5\times5=$ ...
$9\times1=$ ...	$3\times2=$ ...	$9\times6=$ ...	$6\times4=$ ...

Exercise n°:2 : Adding fractions

Example: $\frac{4}{8}+\frac{5}{2}=\frac{4+20}{8}=\frac{24}{8}$

LCM(8,2) = 8

(1) $\frac{8}{9}+\frac{6}{4}=\frac{\dots+\dots}{\dots}=\frac{\dots}{\dots}$

(2) $\frac{9}{1}+\frac{4}{2}=\frac{\dots+\dots}{\dots}=\frac{\dots}{\dots}$

(3) $\frac{6}{6}+\frac{1}{7}=\frac{\dots+\dots}{\dots}=\frac{\dots}{\dots}$

(4) $\frac{4}{4}+\frac{3}{4}=\frac{\dots+\dots}{\dots}=\frac{\dots}{\dots}$

(5) $4+\frac{5}{5}=\frac{\dots+\dots}{\dots}=\frac{\dots}{\dots}$

(6) $\frac{1}{1}+\frac{5}{4}=\frac{\dots+\dots}{\dots}=\frac{\dots}{\dots}$

Answer key	Score
(1) $\frac{86}{36}$ (2) $\frac{22}{2}$ (3) $\frac{48}{42}$ (4) $\frac{7}{4}$ (5) $\frac{25}{5}$ (6) $\frac{9}{4}$	/6

*LCM= **L**east **C**ommon **M**ultiple*

Addition

(With unlike denominators)

Name: ....

School: ....

DAY: 29

Exercise n°:1 : Multiplication review

$8\times6=$ ... $1\times7=$ ... $7\times7=$ ... $4\times4=$ ...

$6\times7=$ ... $3\times4=$ ... $6\times2=$ ... $9\times9=$ ...

Exercise n°:2 : Adding fractions

Example: $\frac{6}{8}+\frac{7}{6}=\frac{18+28}{24}=\frac{46}{24}$

LCM(8,6) = 24

(1) $\frac{1}{1}+\frac{8}{9}=\frac{\ldots+\ldots}{\ldots}=\frac{\ldots}{\ldots}$

(2) $\frac{6}{7}+\frac{7}{4}=\frac{\ldots+\ldots}{\ldots}=\frac{\ldots}{\ldots}$

(3) $\frac{2}{9}+\frac{7}{6}=\frac{\ldots+\ldots}{\ldots}=\frac{\ldots}{\ldots}$

(4) $\frac{9}{1}+\frac{2}{1}=\frac{\ldots+\ldots}{\ldots}=\frac{\ldots}{\ldots}$

(5) $6+\frac{2}{4}=\frac{\ldots+\ldots}{\ldots}=\frac{\ldots}{\ldots}$

(6) $\frac{2}{1}+\frac{4}{1}=\frac{\ldots+\ldots}{\ldots}=\frac{\ldots}{\ldots}$

Answer key	Score
(1) $\frac{17}{9}$ (2) $\frac{73}{28}$ (3) $\frac{25}{18}$ (4) $\frac{11}{1}$ (5) $\frac{26}{4}$ (6) $\frac{6}{1}$	/6

*LCM= **L**east **C**ommon **M**ultiple*

Addition

(With unlike denominators)

Name: ....

School: ....

DAY : 30

Exercise n°:1 : Multiplication review

$6\times7=$ ...	$8\times9=$ ...	$6\times6=$ ...	$3\times3=$ ...
$6\times6=$ ...	$5\times5=$ ...	$6\times7=$ ...	$7\times3=$ ...

Exercise n°:2 : Adding fractions

Example: $\frac{6}{6}+\frac{1}{7}=\frac{42+6}{42}=\frac{48}{42}$

LCM(6,7) = 42

(1) $\frac{2}{5}+\frac{6}{6}=\frac{\dots+\dots}{\dots}=\frac{\dots}{\dots}$

(2) $\frac{6}{6}+\frac{9}{5}=\frac{\dots+\dots}{\dots}=\frac{\dots}{\dots}$

(3) $\frac{7}{7}+\frac{4}{8}=\frac{\dots+\dots}{\dots}=\frac{\dots}{\dots}$

(4) $\frac{3}{1}+\frac{6}{7}=\frac{\dots+\dots}{\dots}=\frac{\dots}{\dots}$

(5) $2+\frac{5}{3}=\frac{\dots+\dots}{\dots}=\frac{\dots}{\dots}$

(6) $\frac{1}{1}+\frac{2}{8}=\frac{\dots+\dots}{\dots}=\frac{\dots}{\dots}$

Answer key	Score
(1) $\frac{42}{30}$ (2) $\frac{84}{30}$ (3) $\frac{84}{56}$ (4) $\frac{27}{7}$ (5) $\frac{11}{3}$ (6) $\frac{10}{8}$	/6

LCM= Least Common Multiple

Subtraction

with like denominators

Name: ....

School: ....

DAY : 31

Exercise n°:1 : Multiplication review

$8\times6=$ ...	$2\times4=$ ...	$5\times4=$ ...	$2\times6=$ ...
$6\times3=$ ...	$3\times3=$ ...	$6\times1=$ ...	$1\times4=$ ...

Exercise n°:2 : Subtracting fractions

Example : $\frac{8}{2}-\frac{4}{2}=\frac{8\ -\ 4}{2}=\frac{4}{2}$ LCM(2,2) = 2

(1) $6-\frac{3}{1}=\frac{\dots\ -\ \dots}{\dots}=\frac{\dots}{\dots}$

(2) $\frac{6}{4}-\frac{4}{4}=\frac{\dots\ -\ \dots}{\dots}=\frac{\dots}{\dots}$

(3) $\frac{6}{3}-\frac{3}{3}=\frac{\dots\ -\ \dots}{\dots}=\frac{\dots}{\dots}$

(4) $\frac{6}{2}-\frac{4}{2}=\frac{\dots\ -\ \dots}{\dots}=\frac{\dots}{\dots}$

(5) $5-\frac{1}{1}=\frac{\dots\ -\ \dots}{\dots}=\frac{\dots}{\dots}$

(6) $\frac{7}{4}-\frac{2}{4}=\frac{\dots\ -\ \dots}{\dots}=\frac{\dots}{\dots}$

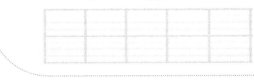

Answer Key	My Score
(1) $\frac{3}{1}$ (2) $\frac{2}{4}$ (3) $\frac{3}{3}$ (4) $\frac{2}{2}$ (5) $\frac{4}{1}$ (6) $\frac{5}{4}$	/6

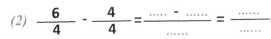

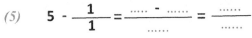

*LCM= **L**east **C**ommon **M**ultiple*

Subtraction

with like denominators

Name: ....

School: ....

DAY: 32

Exercise n°:1 : Multiplication review

$8\times9=\ldots$	$1\times2=\ldots$	$7\times4=\ldots$	$1\times5=\ldots$
$5\times3=\ldots$	$2\times2=\ldots$	$8\times1=\ldots$	$1\times2=\ldots$

Exercise n°:2 : Subtracting fractions

Example : $\frac{8}{1}-\frac{4}{1}=\frac{8-4}{1}=\frac{4}{1}$ LCM(1,1) = 1

(1) $5-\frac{3}{1}=\frac{\ldots\ldots-\ldots\ldots}{\ldots\ldots}=\frac{\ldots\ldots}{\ldots\ldots}$

(2) $\frac{9}{2}-\frac{4}{2}=\frac{\ldots\ldots-\ldots\ldots}{\ldots\ldots}=\frac{\ldots\ldots}{\ldots\ldots}$

(3) $\frac{5}{2}-\frac{3}{2}=\frac{\ldots\ldots-\ldots\ldots}{\ldots\ldots}=\frac{\ldots\ldots}{\ldots\ldots}$

(4) $\frac{8}{3}-\frac{3}{3}=\frac{\ldots\ldots-\ldots\ldots}{\ldots\ldots}=\frac{\ldots\ldots}{\ldots\ldots}$

(5) $7-\frac{4}{1}=\frac{\ldots\ldots-\ldots\ldots}{\ldots\ldots}=\frac{\ldots\ldots}{\ldots\ldots}$

(6) $\frac{7}{1}-\frac{3}{1}=\frac{\ldots\ldots-\ldots\ldots}{\ldots\ldots}=\frac{\ldots\ldots}{\ldots\ldots}$

Answer Key	*My Score*
(1) $\frac{2}{1}$ (2) $\frac{5}{2}$ (3) $\frac{2}{2}$ (4) $\frac{5}{3}$ (5) $\frac{3}{1}$ (6) $\frac{4}{1}$	/6

*LCM= **L**east **C**ommon **M**ultiple*

Subtraction

Name: ....

School: ....

DAY: 33

with unlike denominators

Exercise n°:1 : Multiplication review

$5\times7=$ ...	$1\times2=$ ...	$4\times1=$ ...	$9\times4=$ ...
$4\times2=$ ...	$5\times2=$ ...	$2\times9=$ ...	$7\times2=$ ...

Exercise n°:2 : Subtracting fractions

Example : $\frac{5}{1} - \frac{5}{9} = \frac{45 - 5}{9} = \frac{40}{9}$ LCM(1,9) = 9

(1) $4 - \frac{6}{9} = \frac{\dots - \dots}{\dots} = \frac{\dots}{\dots}$

(2) $\frac{7}{6} - \frac{1}{2} = \frac{\dots - \dots}{\dots} = \frac{\dots}{\dots}$

(3) $\frac{4}{2} - \frac{2}{5} = \frac{\dots - \dots}{\dots} = \frac{\dots}{\dots}$

(4) $\frac{2}{1} - \frac{1}{8} = \frac{\dots - \dots}{\dots} = \frac{\dots}{\dots}$

(5) $4 - \frac{1}{2} = \frac{\dots - \dots}{\dots} = \frac{\dots}{\dots}$

(6) $\frac{5}{2} - \frac{3}{6} = \frac{\dots - \dots}{\dots} = \frac{\dots}{\dots}$

Answer Key	***My Score***
(1) $\frac{30}{9}$ (2) $\frac{4}{6}$ (3) $\frac{16}{10}$ (4) $\frac{15}{8}$ (5) $\frac{7}{2}$ (6) $\frac{12}{6}$	/6

*LCM= **L**east **C**ommon **M**ultiple*

Subtraction

with unlike denominators

Name: ....

School: ....

DAY: 34

Exercise n°:1 : Multiplication review

$7\times4=\ldots$	$4\times6=\ldots$	$5\times2=\ldots$	$2\times2=\ldots$
$9\times1=\ldots$	$5\times1=\ldots$	$2\times1=\ldots$	$6\times6=\ldots$

Exercise n°:2 : Subtracting fractions

Example : $\frac{7}{4}-\frac{1}{2}=\frac{7-2}{4}=\frac{5}{4}$ LCM(4,2) = 4

(1) $9-\frac{7}{8}=\frac{\ldots\ldots-\ldots\ldots}{\ldots\ldots}=\frac{\ldots\ldots}{\ldots\ldots}$

(2) $\frac{4}{3}-\frac{2}{6}=\frac{\ldots\ldots-\ldots\ldots}{\ldots\ldots}=\frac{\ldots\ldots}{\ldots\ldots}$

(3) $\frac{2}{1}-\frac{1}{5}=\frac{\ldots\ldots-\ldots\ldots}{\ldots\ldots}=\frac{\ldots\ldots}{\ldots\ldots}$

(4) $\frac{2}{1}-\frac{4}{5}=\frac{\ldots\ldots-\ldots\ldots}{\ldots\ldots}=\frac{\ldots\ldots}{\ldots\ldots}$

(5) $5-\frac{2}{6}=\frac{\ldots\ldots-\ldots\ldots}{\ldots\ldots}=\frac{\ldots\ldots}{\ldots\ldots}$

(6) $\frac{2}{1}-\frac{2}{8}=\frac{\ldots\ldots-\ldots\ldots}{\ldots\ldots}=\frac{\ldots\ldots}{\ldots\ldots}$

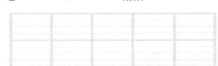

Answer Key	My Score
(1) $\frac{65}{8}$ (2) $\frac{6}{6}$ (3) $\frac{9}{5}$ (4) $\frac{6}{5}$ (5) $\frac{28}{6}$ (6) $\frac{14}{8}$	/6

*LCM= **L**east **C**ommon **M**ultiple*

Subtraction

Name: ....

School: ....

DAY: 35

with unlike denominators

Exercise n°:1 : Multiplication review

$2\times5=$ ...	$1\times8=$ ...	$4\times3=$ ...	$8\times6=$ ...
$8\times1=$ ...	$2\times3=$ ...	$2\times8=$ ...	$9\times8=$ ...

Exercise n°:2 : Subtracting fractions

Example : $\frac{2}{1} - \frac{3}{8} = \frac{16 - 3}{8} = \frac{13}{8}$ LCM(1,8) = 8

(1) $8 - \frac{1}{3} = \frac{\dots\dots - \dots\dots}{\dots\dots} = \frac{\dots\dots}{\dots\dots}$

(2) $\frac{5}{4} - \frac{3}{8} = \frac{\dots\dots - \dots\dots}{\dots\dots} = \frac{\dots\dots}{\dots\dots}$

(3) $\frac{6}{3} - \frac{1}{2} = \frac{\dots\dots - \dots\dots}{\dots\dots} = \frac{\dots\dots}{\dots\dots}$

(4) $\frac{2}{1} - \frac{3}{6} = \frac{\dots\dots - \dots\dots}{\dots\dots} = \frac{\dots\dots}{\dots\dots}$

(5) $4 - \frac{1}{7} = \frac{\dots\dots - \dots\dots}{\dots\dots} = \frac{\dots\dots}{\dots\dots}$

(6) $\frac{2}{1} - \frac{3}{4} = \frac{\dots\dots - \dots\dots}{\dots\dots} = \frac{\dots\dots}{\dots\dots}$

Answer Key	My Score
(1) $\frac{23}{3}$ (2) $\frac{7}{8}$ (3) $\frac{9}{6}$ (4) $\frac{9}{6}$ (5) $\frac{27}{7}$ (6) $\frac{5}{4}$	/6

*LCM= **L**east **C**ommon **M**ultiple*

Subtraction

with unlike denominators

Name: ....

School: ....

DAY: ***36***

Exercise n°:1 : Multiplication review

$3\times9=$ ...	$2\times5=$ ...	$8\times3=$ ...	$6\times9=$ ...
$6\times3=$ ...	$8\times3=$ ...	$5\times3=$ ...	$7\times5=$ ...

Exercise n°:2 : Subtracting fractions

Example : $\frac{3}{2} - \frac{1}{6} = \frac{9-1}{6} = \frac{8}{6}$ LCM(2,6) = 6

(1) $6 - \frac{2}{4} = \frac{\ldots - \ldots}{\ldots} = \frac{\ldots}{\ldots}$

(2) $\frac{9}{1} - \frac{3}{5} = \frac{\ldots - \ldots}{\ldots} = \frac{\ldots}{\ldots}$

(3) $\frac{9}{3} - \frac{3}{8} = \frac{\ldots - \ldots}{\ldots} = \frac{\ldots}{\ldots}$

(4) $\frac{5}{2} - \frac{3}{7} = \frac{\ldots - \ldots}{\ldots} = \frac{\ldots}{\ldots}$

(5) $8 - \frac{2}{3} = \frac{\ldots - \ldots}{\ldots} = \frac{\ldots}{\ldots}$

(6) $\frac{3}{1} - \frac{1}{2} = \frac{\ldots - \ldots}{\ldots} = \frac{\ldots}{\ldots}$

Answer Key	*My Score*
(1) $\frac{22}{4}$ (2) $\frac{42}{5}$ (3) $\frac{63}{24}$ (4) $\frac{29}{14}$ (5) $\frac{22}{3}$ (6) $\frac{5}{2}$	/6

*LCM= **L**east **C**ommon **M**ultiple*

Subtraction

with unlike denominators

Name: ....

School: ....

DAY: 37

Exercise n°:1 : Multiplication review

$6\times4=$ ...	$2\times5=$ ...	$8\times3=$ ...	$4\times8=$ ...
$4\times6=$ ...	$9\times2=$ ...	$2\times2=$ ...	$5\times5=$ ...

Exercise n°:2 : Subtracting fractions

Example : $\frac{6}{2}-\frac{1}{4}=\frac{12-1}{4}=\frac{11}{4}$ LCM(2,4) = 4

(1) $4-\frac{4}{9}=\frac{\ldots\ -\ \ldots}{\ldots}=\frac{\ldots}{\ldots}$

(2) $\frac{4}{1}-\frac{3}{5}=\frac{\ldots\ -\ \ldots}{\ldots}=\frac{\ldots}{\ldots}$

(3) $\frac{8}{2}-\frac{6}{9}=\frac{\ldots\ -\ \ldots}{\ldots}=\frac{\ldots}{\ldots}$

(4) $\frac{2}{1}-\frac{3}{8}=\frac{\ldots\ -\ \ldots}{\ldots}=\frac{\ldots}{\ldots}$

(5) $8-\frac{2}{4}=\frac{\ldots\ -\ \ldots}{\ldots}=\frac{\ldots}{\ldots}$

(6) $\frac{6}{5}-\frac{4}{7}=\frac{\ldots\ -\ \ldots}{\ldots}=\frac{\ldots}{\ldots}$

Answer Key	*My Score*
(1) $\frac{32}{9}$ (2) $\frac{17}{5}$ (3) $\frac{60}{18}$ (4) $\frac{13}{8}$ (5) $\frac{30}{4}$ (6) $\frac{22}{35}$	/6

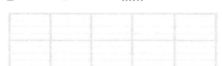

*LCM= **L**east **C**ommon **M**ultiple*

Subtraction

Name: ....

School: ....

DAY: 38

with unlike denominators

Exercise n°:1 : Multiplication review

$6 \times 7 =$ ...	$1 \times 5 =$ ...	$6 \times 4 =$ ...	$6 \times 9 =$ ...
$7 \times 2 =$ ...	$4 \times 8 =$ ...	$6 \times 6 =$ ...	$8 \times 5 =$ ...

Exercise n°:2 : Subtracting fractions

Example : $\frac{6}{1} - \frac{4}{6} = \frac{36\ -\ 4}{6} = \frac{32}{6}$ LCM(1,6) = 6

(1) $7 - \frac{7}{8} = \frac{\ldots\ -\ \ldots}{\ldots} = \frac{\ldots}{\ldots}$

(2) $\frac{7}{1} - \frac{4}{5} = \frac{\ldots\ -\ \ldots}{\ldots} = \frac{\ldots}{\ldots}$

(3) $\frac{9}{8} - \frac{2}{4} = \frac{\ldots\ -\ \ldots}{\ldots} = \frac{\ldots}{\ldots}$

(4) $\frac{6}{2} - \frac{1}{6} = \frac{\ldots\ -\ \ldots}{\ldots} = \frac{\ldots}{\ldots}$

(5) $6 - \frac{1}{5} = \frac{\ldots\ -\ \ldots}{\ldots} = \frac{\ldots}{\ldots}$

(6) $\frac{9}{1} - \frac{4}{5} = \frac{\ldots\ -\ \ldots}{\ldots} = \frac{\ldots}{\ldots}$

Answer Key	*My Score*
(1) $\frac{49}{8}$ (2) $\frac{31}{5}$ (3) $\frac{5}{8}$ (4) $\frac{17}{6}$ (5) $\frac{29}{5}$ (6) $\frac{41}{5}$	/6

*LCM= **L**east **C**ommon **M**ultiple*

Subtraction

Name: ....

School: ....

DAY: 39

with unlike denominators

Exercise n°:1 : Multiplication review

$4 \times 2 = \ldots$	$1 \times 7 = \ldots$	$9 \times 2 = \ldots$	$5 \times 2 = \ldots$
$5 \times 3 = \ldots$	$4 \times 1 = \ldots$	$8 \times 5 = \ldots$	$5 \times 7 = \ldots$

Exercise n°:2 : Subtracting fractions

Example : $\frac{4}{1} - \frac{3}{5} = \frac{20 - 3}{5} = \frac{17}{5}$ LCM(1,5) = 5

(1) $5 - \frac{1}{3} = \frac{\ldots - \ldots}{\ldots} = \frac{\ldots}{\ldots}$

(2) $\frac{2}{1} - \frac{2}{7} = \frac{\ldots - \ldots}{\ldots} = \frac{\ldots}{\ldots}$

(3) $\frac{2}{1} - \frac{3}{4} = \frac{\ldots - \ldots}{\ldots} = \frac{\ldots}{\ldots}$

(4) $\frac{8}{2} - \frac{1}{2} = \frac{\ldots - \ldots}{\ldots} = \frac{\ldots}{\ldots}$

(5) $9 - \frac{5}{8} = \frac{\ldots - \ldots}{\ldots} = \frac{\ldots}{\ldots}$

(6) $\frac{9}{2} - \frac{4}{5} = \frac{\ldots - \ldots}{\ldots} = \frac{\ldots}{\ldots}$

Answer Key	My Score
(1) $\frac{14}{3}$ (2) $\frac{12}{7}$ (3) $\frac{5}{4}$ (4) $\frac{7}{2}$ (5) $\frac{67}{8}$ (6) $\frac{37}{10}$	/6

*LCM= **L**east **C**ommon **M**ultiple*

Subtraction

Name: ....

School: ....

DAY: 40

with unlike denominators

Exercise n°:1 : Multiplication review

$2\times9=$ ...	$1\times9=$ ...	$4\times2=$ ...	$2\times2=$ ...
$4\times3=$ ...	$6\times1=$ ...	$6\times2=$ ...	$7\times9=$ ...

Exercise n°:2 : Subtracting fractions

Example : $\frac{2}{1} - \frac{1}{2} = \frac{4-1}{2} = \frac{3}{2}$ LCM(1,2) = 2

(1) $4 - \frac{2}{3} = \frac{\dots - \dots}{\dots} = \frac{\dots}{\dots}$

(2) $\frac{9}{6} - \frac{2}{9} = \frac{\dots - \dots}{\dots} = \frac{\dots}{\dots}$

(3) $\frac{2}{1} - \frac{3}{6} = \frac{\dots - \dots}{\dots} = \frac{\dots}{\dots}$

(4) $\frac{6}{3} - \frac{3}{5} = \frac{\dots - \dots}{\dots} = \frac{\dots}{\dots}$

(5) $4 - \frac{3}{5} = \frac{\dots - \dots}{\dots} = \frac{\dots}{\dots}$

(6) $\frac{8}{7} - \frac{3}{4} = \frac{\dots - \dots}{\dots} = \frac{\dots}{\dots}$

Answer Key	My Score
(1) $\frac{10}{3}$ (2) $\frac{23}{18}$ (3) $\frac{9}{6}$ (4) $\frac{21}{15}$ (5) $\frac{17}{5}$ (6) $\frac{11}{28}$	/6

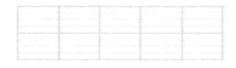

LCM= **L**east **C**ommon **M**ultiple

Subtraction

with unlike denominators

Name: ....

School: ....

DAY: 41

Exercise n°:1 : Multiplication review

$9\times3=$ ...	$8\times6=$ ...	$4\times3=$ ...	$7\times7=$ ...
$6\times1=$ ...	$2\times1=$ ...	$2\times7=$ ...	$5\times6=$ ...

Exercise n°:2 : Subtracting fractions

Example : $\frac{9}{8} - \frac{1}{7} = \frac{63 - 8}{56} = \frac{55}{56}$ LCM(8,7) = 56

(1) $6 - \frac{2}{3} = \frac{\dots - \dots}{\dots} = \frac{\dots}{\dots}$

(2) $\frac{3}{2} - \frac{3}{6} = \frac{\dots - \dots}{\dots} = \frac{\dots}{\dots}$

(3) $\frac{7}{1} - \frac{1}{2} = \frac{\dots - \dots}{\dots} = \frac{\dots}{\dots}$

(4) $\frac{2}{1} - \frac{3}{7} = \frac{\dots - \dots}{\dots} = \frac{\dots}{\dots}$

(5) $4 - \frac{1}{4} = \frac{\dots - \dots}{\dots} = \frac{\dots}{\dots}$

(6) $\frac{2}{1} - \frac{1}{4} = \frac{\dots - \dots}{\dots} = \frac{\dots}{\dots}$

Answer Key	My Score
(1) $\frac{16}{3}$ (2) $\frac{6}{6}$ (3) $\frac{13}{2}$ (4) $\frac{11}{7}$ (5) $\frac{15}{4}$ (6) $\frac{7}{4}$	/6

LCM= Least Common Multiple

Subtraction

Name: ....

School: ....

DAY: 42

with unlike denominators

Exercise n°:1 : Multiplication review

$8\times4 = \ldots$ $\quad$ $2\times7 = \ldots$ $\quad$ $5\times4 = \ldots$ $\quad$ $6\times3 = \ldots$

$2\times1 = \ldots$ $\quad$ $8\times1 = \ldots$ $\quad$ $5\times3 = \ldots$ $\quad$ $7\times7 = \ldots$

Exercise n°:2 : Subtracting fractions

Example : $\frac{8}{2} - \frac{2}{6} = \frac{24 - 2}{6} = \frac{22}{6}$ LCM(2,6) = 6

(1) $2 - \frac{3}{5} = \frac{\ldots - \ldots}{\ldots} = \frac{\ldots}{\ldots}$

(2) $\frac{4}{2} - \frac{4}{7} = \frac{\ldots - \ldots}{\ldots} = \frac{\ldots}{\ldots}$

(3) $\frac{3}{1} - \frac{1}{8} = \frac{\ldots - \ldots}{\ldots} = \frac{\ldots}{\ldots}$

(4) $\frac{5}{4} - \frac{3}{4} = \frac{\ldots - \ldots}{\ldots} = \frac{\ldots}{\ldots}$

(5) $5 - \frac{2}{4} = \frac{\ldots - \ldots}{\ldots} = \frac{\ldots}{\ldots}$

(6) $\frac{3}{2} - \frac{6}{8} = \frac{\ldots - \ldots}{\ldots} = \frac{\ldots}{\ldots}$

Answer Key	My Score
(1) $\frac{7}{5}$ (2) $\frac{20}{14}$ (3) $\frac{23}{8}$ (4) $\frac{2}{4}$ (5) $\frac{18}{4}$ (6) $\frac{6}{8}$	/6

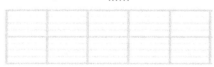

*LCM= **L**east **C**ommon **M**ultiple*

Subtraction

with unlike denominators

Name: ....

School: ....

DAY: 43

Exercise n°:1 : Multiplication review

$4 \times 6 =$ ...	$1 \times 9 =$ ...	$5 \times 1 =$ ...	$4 \times 6 =$ ...
$9 \times 1 =$ ...	$2 \times 5 =$ ...	$9 \times 4 =$ ...	$2 \times 9 =$ ...

Exercise n°:2 : Subtracting fractions

Example : $\frac{4}{1} - \frac{2}{4} = \frac{16 - 2}{4} = \frac{14}{4}$ LCM(1,4) = 4

(1) $9 - \frac{4}{5} = \frac{\ldots - \ldots}{\ldots} = \frac{\ldots}{\ldots}$

(2) $\frac{6}{3} - \frac{1}{9} = \frac{\ldots - \ldots}{\ldots} = \frac{\ldots}{\ldots}$

(3) $\frac{6}{5} - \frac{1}{2} = \frac{\ldots - \ldots}{\ldots} = \frac{\ldots}{\ldots}$

(4) $\frac{9}{6} - \frac{3}{7} = \frac{\ldots - \ldots}{\ldots} = \frac{\ldots}{\ldots}$

(5) $5 - \frac{2}{7} = \frac{\ldots - \ldots}{\ldots} = \frac{\ldots}{\ldots}$

(6) $\frac{3}{1} - \frac{1}{2} = \frac{\ldots - \ldots}{\ldots} = \frac{\ldots}{\ldots}$

Answer Key	My Score
(1) $\frac{41}{5}$ (2) $\frac{17}{9}$ (3) $\frac{7}{10}$ (4) $\frac{45}{42}$ (5) $\frac{33}{7}$ (6) $\frac{5}{2}$	/6

*LCM= **L**east **C**ommon **M**ultiple*

Subtraction

with unlike denominators

Name: ....

School: ....

DAY: 44

Exercise n°:1 : Multiplication review

$5\times 9 =$ ...	$1\times 6 =$ ...	$5\times 3 =$ ...	$3\times 7 =$ ...
$3\times 1 =$ ...	$4\times 3 =$ ...	$2\times 3 =$ ...	$6\times 6 =$ ...

Exercise n°:2 : Subtracting fractions

Example : $\frac{5}{1} - \frac{2}{3} = \frac{15 - 2}{3} = \frac{13}{3}$ LCM(1,3) = 3

(1) $3 - \frac{1}{5} = \frac{\dots\ -\ \dots}{\dots} = \frac{\dots}{\dots}$

(2) $\frac{9}{2} - \frac{3}{6} = \frac{\dots\ -\ \dots}{\dots} = \frac{\dots}{\dots}$

(3) $\frac{7}{3} - \frac{1}{4} = \frac{\dots\ -\ \dots}{\dots} = \frac{\dots}{\dots}$

(4) $\frac{2}{1} - \frac{5}{9} = \frac{\dots\ -\ \dots}{\dots} = \frac{\dots}{\dots}$

(5) $5 - \frac{5}{6} = \frac{\dots\ -\ \dots}{\dots} = \frac{\dots}{\dots}$

(6) $\frac{5}{2} - \frac{6}{8} = \frac{\dots\ -\ \dots}{\dots} = \frac{\dots}{\dots}$

Answer Key	*My Score*
(1) $\frac{14}{5}$ (2) $\frac{24}{6}$ (3) $\frac{25}{12}$ (4) $\frac{13}{9}$ (5) $\frac{25}{6}$ (6) $\frac{14}{8}$	/6

*LCM= **L**east **C**ommon **M**ultiple*

Subtraction

Name: ....

School: ....

DAY: 45

with unlike denominators

Exercise n°:1 : Multiplication review

$9\times7=$ ...	$2\times5=$ ...	$4\times3=$ ...	$8\times4=$ ...
$4\times1=$ ...	$2\times2=$ ...	$8\times4=$ ...	$7\times5=$ ...

Exercise n°:2 : Subtracting fractions

Example : $\frac{9}{2}-\frac{7}{8}=\frac{36-7}{8}=\frac{29}{8}$ LCM(2,8) = 8

(1) $4-\frac{1}{2}=\frac{\dots\dots-\dots\dots}{\dots\dots}=\frac{\dots\dots}{\dots\dots}$

(2) $\frac{7}{1}-\frac{3}{5}=\frac{\dots\dots-\dots\dots}{\dots\dots}=\frac{\dots\dots}{\dots\dots}$

(3) $\frac{4}{2}-\frac{1}{2}=\frac{\dots\dots-\dots\dots}{\dots\dots}=\frac{\dots\dots}{\dots\dots}$

(4) $\frac{8}{6}-\frac{2}{3}=\frac{\dots\dots-\dots\dots}{\dots\dots}=\frac{\dots\dots}{\dots\dots}$

(5) $4-\frac{5}{9}=\frac{\dots\dots-\dots\dots}{\dots\dots}=\frac{\dots\dots}{\dots\dots}$

(6) $\frac{2}{1}-\frac{1}{2}=\frac{\dots\dots-\dots\dots}{\dots\dots}=\frac{\dots\dots}{\dots\dots}$

Answer Key	My Score
(1) $\frac{7}{2}$ (2) $\frac{32}{5}$ (3) $\frac{3}{2}$ (4) $\frac{4}{6}$ (5) $\frac{31}{9}$ (6) $\frac{3}{2}$	/6

*LCM= **L**east **C**ommon **M**ultiple*

Subtraction

with unlike denominators

Name: ....

School: ....

DAY: 46

Exercise n°:1 : Multiplication review

$9\times8=$ ...	$8\times8=$ ...	$2\times7=$ ...	$3\times5=$ ...
$6\times4=$ ...	$7\times2=$ ...	$3\times3=$ ...	$4\times8=$ ...

Exercise n°:2 : Subtracting fractions

Example : $\frac{9}{8}-\frac{2}{3}=\frac{27-16}{24}=\frac{11}{24}$ LCM(8,3) = 24

(1) $6-\frac{2}{8}=\frac{\ldots\ -\ \ldots}{\ldots}=\frac{\ldots}{\ldots}$

(2) $\frac{8}{5}-\frac{7}{8}=\frac{\ldots\ -\ \ldots}{\ldots}=\frac{\ldots}{\ldots}$

(3) $\frac{5}{2}-\frac{4}{7}=\frac{\ldots\ -\ \ldots}{\ldots}=\frac{\ldots}{\ldots}$

(4) $\frac{3}{1}-\frac{7}{8}=\frac{\ldots\ -\ \ldots}{\ldots}=\frac{\ldots}{\ldots}$

(5) $2-\frac{4}{6}=\frac{\ldots\ -\ \ldots}{\ldots}=\frac{\ldots}{\ldots}$

(6) $\frac{5}{1}-\frac{1}{3}=\frac{\ldots\ -\ \ldots}{\ldots}=\frac{\ldots}{\ldots}$

Answer Key	My Score
(1) $\frac{46}{8}$ (2) $\frac{29}{40}$ (3) $\frac{27}{14}$ (4) $\frac{17}{8}$ (5) $\frac{8}{6}$ (6) $\frac{14}{3}$	/6

*LCM= **L**east **C**ommon **M**ultiple*

Subtraction

Name: ....

School: ....

DAY : 47

with unlike denominators

Exercise n°:1 : Multiplication review

$3\times4=$ ...	$1\times2=$ ...	$9\times1=$ ...	$5\times3=$ ...
$6\times6=$ ...	$7\times1=$ ...	$9\times5=$ ...	$4\times2=$ ...

Exercise n°:2 : Subtracting fractions

Example : $\frac{3}{1} - \frac{1}{5} = \frac{15 - 1}{5} = \frac{14}{5}$ LCM(1,5) = 5

(1) $6 - \frac{1}{2} = \frac{\dots - \dots}{\dots} = \frac{\dots}{\dots}$

(2) $\frac{4}{1} - \frac{1}{2} = \frac{\dots - \dots}{\dots} = \frac{\dots}{\dots}$

(3) $\frac{3}{1} - \frac{6}{7} = \frac{\dots - \dots}{\dots} = \frac{\dots}{\dots}$

(4) $\frac{9}{3} - \frac{4}{9} = \frac{\dots - \dots}{\dots} = \frac{\dots}{\dots}$

(5) $9 - \frac{1}{2} = \frac{\dots - \dots}{\dots} = \frac{\dots}{\dots}$

(6) $\frac{4}{2} - \frac{5}{6} = \frac{\dots - \dots}{\dots} = \frac{\dots}{\dots}$

Answer Key	My Score
(1) $\frac{11}{2}$ (2) $\frac{7}{2}$ (3) $\frac{15}{7}$ (4) $\frac{23}{9}$ (5) $\frac{17}{2}$ (6) $\frac{7}{6}$	/6

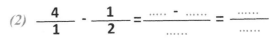

*LCM= **L**east **C**ommon **M**ultiple*

Subtraction

with unlike denominators

Name: ....

School: ....

DAY : 48

Exercise n°:1 : Multiplication review

$2\times9=$ ...	$1\times4=$ ...	$7\times2=$ ...	$5\times8=$ ...
$7\times1=$ ...	$2\times3=$ ...	$9\times5=$ ...	$7\times4=$ ...

Exercise n°:2 : Subtracting fractions

Example : $\frac{2}{1}-\frac{4}{5}=\frac{10-4}{5}=\frac{6}{5}$ LCM(1,5) = 5

(1) $7-\frac{1}{9}=\frac{\ldots\ -\ \ldots}{\ldots}=\frac{\ldots}{\ldots}$

(2) $\frac{9}{4}-\frac{2}{4}=\frac{\ldots\ -\ \ldots}{\ldots}=\frac{\ldots}{\ldots}$

(3) $\frac{8}{3}-\frac{1}{2}=\frac{\ldots\ -\ \ldots}{\ldots}=\frac{\ldots}{\ldots}$

(4) $\frac{9}{7}-\frac{1}{7}=\frac{\ldots\ -\ \ldots}{\ldots}=\frac{\ldots}{\ldots}$

(5) $7-\frac{1}{3}=\frac{\ldots\ -\ \ldots}{\ldots}=\frac{\ldots}{\ldots}$

(6) $\frac{2}{1}-\frac{3}{6}=\frac{\ldots\ -\ \ldots}{\ldots}=\frac{\ldots}{\ldots}$

Answer Key	My Score
(1) $\frac{62}{9}$ (2) $\frac{7}{4}$ (3) $\frac{13}{6}$ (4) $\frac{8}{7}$ (5) $\frac{20}{3}$ (6) $\frac{9}{6}$	/6

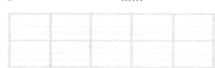

LCM= Least Common Multiple

Subtraction

with unlike denominators

Name: ....

School: ....

DAY: 49

Exercise n°:1 : Multiplication review

$8\times3 =$ ...	$4\times6 =$ ...	$4\times5 =$ ...	$5\times7 =$ ...
$6\times1 =$ ...	$2\times5 =$ ...	$5\times5 =$ ...	$4\times6 =$ ...

Exercise n°:2 : Subtracting fractions

Example : $\frac{8}{4} - \frac{3}{5} = \frac{40 - 12}{20} = \frac{28}{20}$ LCM(4,5) = 20

(1) $6 - \frac{2}{3} = \frac{\ldots - \ldots}{\ldots} = \frac{\ldots}{\ldots}$

(2) $\frac{3}{1} - \frac{5}{6} = \frac{\ldots - \ldots}{\ldots} = \frac{\ldots}{\ldots}$

(3) $\frac{7}{5} - \frac{1}{2} = \frac{\ldots - \ldots}{\ldots} = \frac{\ldots}{\ldots}$

(4) $\frac{5}{4} - \frac{2}{3} = \frac{\ldots - \ldots}{\ldots} = \frac{\ldots}{\ldots}$

(5) $4 - \frac{1}{2} = \frac{\ldots - \ldots}{\ldots} = \frac{\ldots}{\ldots}$

(6) $\frac{3}{2} - \frac{1}{2} = \frac{\ldots - \ldots}{\ldots} = \frac{\ldots}{\ldots}$

Answer Key	My Score
(1) $\frac{16}{3}$ (2) $\frac{13}{6}$ (3) $\frac{9}{10}$ (4) $\frac{7}{12}$ (5) $\frac{7}{2}$ (6) $\frac{2}{2}$	/6

LCM= Least Common Multiple

Subtraction

Name: ....

School: ....

DAY: 50

with unlike denominators

Exercise n°:1 : Multiplication review

$6\times6=\ldots$	$1\times5=\ldots$	$8\times3=\ldots$	$2\times4=\ldots$
$7\times3=\ldots$	$6\times2=\ldots$	$7\times2=\ldots$	$9\times5=\ldots$

Exercise n°:2 : Subtracting fractions

Example : $\frac{6}{1}-\frac{1}{2}=\frac{12-1}{2}=\frac{11}{2}$ LCM(1,2) = 2

(1) $7-\frac{1}{7}=\frac{\ldots\ldots-\ldots\ldots}{\ldots\ldots}=\frac{\ldots\ldots}{\ldots\ldots}$

(2) $\frac{6}{3}-\frac{3}{5}=\frac{\ldots\ldots-\ldots\ldots}{\ldots\ldots}=\frac{\ldots\ldots}{\ldots\ldots}$

(3) $\frac{4}{2}-\frac{3}{6}=\frac{\ldots\ldots-\ldots\ldots}{\ldots\ldots}=\frac{\ldots\ldots}{\ldots\ldots}$

(4) $\frac{7}{5}-\frac{2}{3}=\frac{\ldots\ldots-\ldots\ldots}{\ldots\ldots}=\frac{\ldots\ldots}{\ldots\ldots}$

(5) $8-\frac{4}{5}=\frac{\ldots\ldots-\ldots\ldots}{\ldots\ldots}=\frac{\ldots\ldots}{\ldots\ldots}$

(6) $\frac{5}{2}-\frac{1}{2}=\frac{\ldots\ldots-\ldots\ldots}{\ldots\ldots}=\frac{\ldots\ldots}{\ldots\ldots}$

Answer Key	*My Score*
(1) $\frac{48}{7}$ (2) $\frac{21}{15}$ (3) $\frac{9}{6}$ (4) $\frac{11}{15}$ (5) $\frac{36}{5}$ (6) $\frac{4}{2}$	/6

*LCM= **L**east **C**ommon **M**ultiple*

Subtraction

Name: ....

School: ....

DAY: 51

with unlike denominators

Exercise n°:1 : Multiplication review

$9\times9=\ldots$	$2\times4=\ldots$	$3\times2=\ldots$	$3\times5=\ldots$
$6\times1=\ldots$	$2\times3=\ldots$	$2\times3=\ldots$	$8\times4=\ldots$

Exercise n°:2 : Subtracting fractions

Example : $\frac{9}{2} - \frac{2}{3} = \frac{27\ -\ 4}{6} = \frac{23}{6}$ LCM(2,3) = 6

(1) $6 - \frac{2}{3} = \frac{\ldots\ -\ \ldots}{\ldots} = \frac{\ldots}{\ldots}$

(2) $\frac{9}{4} - \frac{2}{4} = \frac{\ldots\ -\ \ldots}{\ldots} = \frac{\ldots}{\ldots}$

(3) $\frac{5}{3} - \frac{1}{2} = \frac{\ldots\ -\ \ldots}{\ldots} = \frac{\ldots}{\ldots}$

(4) $\frac{2}{1} - \frac{1}{6} = \frac{\ldots\ -\ \ldots}{\ldots} = \frac{\ldots}{\ldots}$

(5) $3 - \frac{1}{3} = \frac{\ldots\ -\ \ldots}{\ldots} = \frac{\ldots}{\ldots}$

(6) $\frac{2}{1} - \frac{1}{4} = \frac{\ldots\ -\ \ldots}{\ldots} = \frac{\ldots}{\ldots}$

Answer Key	My Score
(1) $\frac{16}{3}$ (2) $\frac{7}{4}$ (3) $\frac{7}{6}$ (4) $\frac{11}{6}$ (5) $\frac{8}{3}$ (6) $\frac{7}{4}$	/6

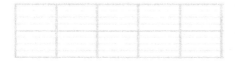

*LCM= **L**east **C**ommon **M**ultiple*

Subtraction

with unlike denominators

Name: ....

School: ....

DAY: 52

Exercise n°:1 : Multiplication review

$4\times6=$ ...	$2\times4=$ ...	$6\times2=$ ...	$7\times8=$ ...
$3\times5=$ ...	$6\times2=$ ...	$7\times7=$ ...	$5\times4=$ ...

Exercise n°:2 : Subtracting fractions

Example : $\frac{4}{2}-\frac{1}{7}=\frac{28\ -\ 2}{14}=\frac{26}{14}$ LCM(2,7) = 14

(1) $3-\frac{3}{8}=\frac{\dots\ -\ \dots}{\dots}=\frac{\dots}{\dots}$

(2) $\frac{6}{2}-\frac{2}{4}=\frac{\dots\ -\ \dots}{\dots}=\frac{\dots}{\dots}$

(3) $\frac{8}{2}-\frac{5}{6}=\frac{\dots\ -\ \dots}{\dots}=\frac{\dots}{\dots}$

(4) $\frac{7}{3}-\frac{6}{9}=\frac{\dots\ -\ \dots}{\dots}=\frac{\dots}{\dots}$

(5) $6-\frac{8}{9}=\frac{\dots\ -\ \dots}{\dots}=\frac{\dots}{\dots}$

(6) $\frac{5}{4}-\frac{3}{5}=\frac{\dots\ -\ \dots}{\dots}=\frac{\dots}{\dots}$

Answer Key	*My Score*
(1) $\frac{21}{8}$ (2) $\frac{10}{4}$ (3) $\frac{19}{6}$ (4) $\frac{15}{9}$ (5) $\frac{46}{9}$ (6) $\frac{13}{20}$	/6

*LCM= **L**east **C**ommon **M**ultiple*

Subtraction

Name: ....

School: ....

DAY: 53

with unlike denominators

Exercise n°:1 : Multiplication review

$2\times8=$ ...	$1\times7=$ ...	$8\times4=$ ...	$7\times6=$ ...
$3\times6=$ ...	$7\times3=$ ...	$4\times7=$ ...	$7\times7=$ ...

Exercise n°:2 : Subtracting fractions

Example : $\frac{2}{1}-\frac{6}{7}=\frac{14-6}{7}=\frac{8}{7}$ LCM(1,7) = 7

(1) $3-\frac{2}{6}=\frac{\dots\dots-\dots\dots}{\dots\dots}=\frac{\dots\dots}{\dots\dots}$

(2) $\frac{8}{7}-\frac{4}{7}=\frac{\dots\dots-\dots\dots}{\dots\dots}=\frac{\dots\dots}{\dots\dots}$

(3) $\frac{6}{3}-\frac{6}{7}=\frac{\dots\dots-\dots\dots}{\dots\dots}=\frac{\dots\dots}{\dots\dots}$

(4) $\frac{4}{3}-\frac{1}{4}=\frac{\dots\dots-\dots\dots}{\dots\dots}=\frac{\dots\dots}{\dots\dots}$

(5) $8-\frac{1}{4}=\frac{\dots\dots-\dots\dots}{\dots\dots}=\frac{\dots\dots}{\dots\dots}$

(6) $\frac{6}{4}-\frac{1}{9}=\frac{\dots\dots-\dots\dots}{\dots\dots}=\frac{\dots\dots}{\dots\dots}$

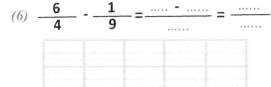

Answer Key	My Score
(1) $\frac{16}{6}$ (2) $\frac{4}{7}$ (3) $\frac{24}{21}$ (4) $\frac{13}{12}$ (5) $\frac{31}{4}$ (6) $\frac{50}{36}$	/6

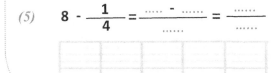

*LCM= **L**east **C**ommon **M**ultiple*

Subtraction

with unlike denominators

Name: ....

School: ....

DAY: 54

Exercise n°:1 : Multiplication review

$8 \times 8 = \ldots$	$5 \times 5 = \ldots$	$4 \times 2 = \ldots$	$2 \times 7 = \ldots$
$4 \times 3 = \ldots$	$6 \times 6 = \ldots$	$9 \times 2 = \ldots$	$8 \times 5 = \ldots$

Exercise n°:2 : Subtracting fractions

Example : $\frac{8}{5} - \frac{1}{2} = \frac{16 - 5}{10} = \frac{11}{10}$ LCM(5,2) = 10

(1) $4 - \frac{4}{7} = \frac{\ldots - \ldots}{\ldots} = \frac{\ldots}{\ldots}$

(2) $\frac{8}{7} - \frac{2}{5} = \frac{\ldots - \ldots}{\ldots} = \frac{\ldots}{\ldots}$

(3) $\frac{7}{6} - \frac{3}{6} = \frac{\ldots - \ldots}{\ldots} = \frac{\ldots}{\ldots}$

(4) $\frac{9}{7} - \frac{2}{3} = \frac{\ldots - \ldots}{\ldots} = \frac{\ldots}{\ldots}$

(5) $4 - \frac{3}{4} = \frac{\ldots - \ldots}{\ldots} = \frac{\ldots}{\ldots}$

(6) $\frac{2}{1} - \frac{3}{5} = \frac{\ldots - \ldots}{\ldots} = \frac{\ldots}{\ldots}$

Answer Key	***My Score***
(1) $\frac{24}{7}$ (2) $\frac{26}{35}$ (3) $\frac{4}{6}$ (4) $\frac{13}{21}$ (5) $\frac{13}{4}$ (6) $\frac{7}{5}$	/6

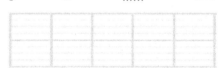

*LCM= **L**east **C**ommon **M**ultiple*

Subtraction

Name: ……………………

School: ……………………

DAY: 55

with unlike denominators

Exercise n°:1 : Multiplication review

$9\times5=\ldots$	$8\times6=\ldots$	$6\times5=\ldots$	$7\times4=\ldots$
$3\times1=\ldots$	$8\times3=\ldots$	$9\times7=\ldots$	$2\times6=\ldots$

Exercise n°:2 : Subtracting fractions

Example : $\frac{9}{8}-\frac{6}{7}=\frac{63-48}{56}=\frac{15}{56}$ LCM(8,7) = 56

(1) $3-\frac{3}{5}=\frac{\ldots-\ldots}{\ldots}=\frac{\ldots}{\ldots}$

(2) $\frac{5}{4}-\frac{5}{6}=\frac{\ldots-\ldots}{\ldots}=\frac{\ldots}{\ldots}$

(3) $\frac{4}{3}-\frac{1}{8}=\frac{\ldots-\ldots}{\ldots}=\frac{\ldots}{\ldots}$

(4) $\frac{9}{3}-\frac{1}{3}=\frac{\ldots-\ldots}{\ldots}=\frac{\ldots}{\ldots}$

(5) $6-\frac{2}{6}=\frac{\ldots-\ldots}{\ldots}=\frac{\ldots}{\ldots}$

(6) $\frac{8}{4}-\frac{1}{2}=\frac{\ldots-\ldots}{\ldots}=\frac{\ldots}{\ldots}$

Answer Key	My Score
(1) $\frac{12}{5}$ (2) $\frac{5}{12}$ (3) $\frac{29}{24}$ (4) $\frac{8}{3}$ (5) $\frac{34}{6}$ (6) $\frac{6}{4}$	/6

*LCM= **L**east **C**ommon **M**ultiple*

Subtraction

with unlike denominators

Name: ....

School: ....

DAY: 56

Exercise n°:1 : Multiplication review

$3\times3=$ ...	$1\times8=$ ...	$6\times1=$ ...	$3\times3=$ ...
$2\times3=$ ...	$8\times2=$ ...	$5\times3=$ ...	$3\times8=$ ...

Exercise n°:2 : Subtracting fractions

Example : $\frac{3}{1} - \frac{1}{3} = \frac{9\ -\ 1}{3} = \frac{8}{3}$ LCM(1,3) = 3

(1) $2 - \frac{3}{9} = \frac{\ldots\ -\ \ldots}{\ldots} = \frac{\ldots}{\ldots}$

(2) $\frac{3}{2} - \frac{1}{8} = \frac{\ldots\ -\ \ldots}{\ldots} = \frac{\ldots}{\ldots}$

(3) $\frac{3}{2} - \frac{3}{8} = \frac{\ldots\ -\ \ldots}{\ldots} = \frac{\ldots}{\ldots}$

(4) $\frac{5}{2} - \frac{1}{2} = \frac{\ldots\ -\ \ldots}{\ldots} = \frac{\ldots}{\ldots}$

(5) $6 - \frac{1}{2} = \frac{\ldots\ -\ \ldots}{\ldots} = \frac{\ldots}{\ldots}$

(6) $\frac{6}{2} - \frac{1}{4} = \frac{\ldots\ -\ \ldots}{\ldots} = \frac{\ldots}{\ldots}$

Answer Key	My Score
(1) $\frac{15}{9}$ (2) $\frac{11}{8}$ (3) $\frac{9}{8}$ (4) $\frac{4}{2}$ (5) $\frac{11}{2}$ (6) $\frac{11}{4}$	/6

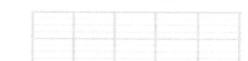

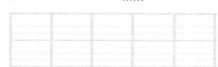

*LCM= **L**east **C**ommon **M**ultiple*

Subtraction

Name: ....

School: ....

DAY: 57

with unlike denominators

Exercise n°:1 : Multiplication review

$5\times4=$ ...	$2\times2=$ ...	$9\times1=$ ...	$7\times6=$ ...
$6\times6=$ ...	$8\times3=$ ...	$3\times7=$ ...	$7\times2=$ ...

Exercise n°:2 : Subtracting fractions

Example : $\frac{5}{2}-\frac{4}{7}=\frac{35-8}{14}=\frac{27}{14}$ LCM(2,7) = 14

(1) $6-\frac{1}{3}=\frac{\ldots\ -\ \ldots}{\ldots}=\frac{\ldots}{\ldots}$

(2) $\frac{4}{2}-\frac{1}{2}=\frac{\ldots\ -\ \ldots}{\ldots}=\frac{\ldots}{\ldots}$

(3) $\frac{6}{3}-\frac{6}{8}=\frac{\ldots\ -\ \ldots}{\ldots}=\frac{\ldots}{\ldots}$

(4) $\frac{3}{1}-\frac{3}{7}=\frac{\ldots\ -\ \ldots}{\ldots}=\frac{\ldots}{\ldots}$

(5) $9-\frac{3}{5}=\frac{\ldots\ -\ \ldots}{\ldots}=\frac{\ldots}{\ldots}$

(6) $\frac{9}{8}-\frac{2}{7}=\frac{\ldots\ -\ \ldots}{\ldots}=\frac{\ldots}{\ldots}$

Answer Key	*My Score*
(1) $\frac{17}{3}$ (2) $\frac{3}{2}$ (3) $\frac{30}{24}$ (4) $\frac{18}{7}$ (5) $\frac{42}{5}$ (6) $\frac{47}{56}$	/6

*LCM= **L**east **C**ommon **M**ultiple*

Subtraction

with unlike denominators

Name: ....

School: ....

DAY : 58

Exercise n°:1 : Multiplication review

$5\times7=$ ...	$1\times9=$ ...	$6\times8=$ ...	$6\times9=$ ...
$5\times6=$ ...	$9\times4=$ ...	$4\times6=$ ...	$3\times9=$ ...

Exercise n°:2 : Subtracting fractions

Example : $\frac{5}{1} - \frac{1}{6} = \frac{30 - 1}{6} = \frac{29}{6}$ LCM(1,6) = 6

(1) $5 - \frac{6}{9} = \frac{\ldots - \ldots}{\ldots} = \frac{\ldots}{\ldots}$

(2) $\frac{7}{6} - \frac{8}{9} = \frac{\ldots - \ldots}{\ldots} = \frac{\ldots}{\ldots}$

(3) $\frac{9}{4} - \frac{6}{9} = \frac{\ldots - \ldots}{\ldots} = \frac{\ldots}{\ldots}$

(4) $\frac{4}{1} - \frac{1}{5} = \frac{\ldots - \ldots}{\ldots} = \frac{\ldots}{\ldots}$

(5) $6 - \frac{1}{5} = \frac{\ldots - \ldots}{\ldots} = \frac{\ldots}{\ldots}$

(6) $\frac{6}{5} - \frac{2}{4} = \frac{\ldots - \ldots}{\ldots} = \frac{\ldots}{\ldots}$

Answer Key	My Score
(1) $\frac{39}{9}$ (2) $\frac{5}{18}$ (3) $\frac{57}{36}$ (4) $\frac{19}{5}$ (5) $\frac{29}{5}$ (6) $\frac{14}{20}$	/6

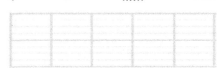

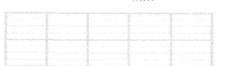

LCM= Least Common Multiple

Subtraction

with unlike denominators

Name: ....

School: ....

DAY: 59

Exercise n°:1 : Multiplication review

$6\times5=\ldots$	$3\times3=\ldots$	$6\times2=\ldots$	$6\times4=\ldots$
$7\times8=\ldots$	$9\times3=\ldots$	$6\times2=\ldots$	$7\times3=\ldots$

Exercise n°:2 : Subtracting fractions

Example : $\frac{6}{3}-\frac{2}{6}=\frac{12-2}{6}=\frac{10}{6}$ LCM(3,6) = 6

(1) $7-\frac{2}{7}=\frac{\ldots\ldots-\ldots\ldots}{\ldots\ldots}=\frac{\ldots\ldots}{\ldots\ldots}$

(2) $\frac{5}{3}-\frac{2}{3}=\frac{\ldots\ldots-\ldots\ldots}{\ldots\ldots}=\frac{\ldots\ldots}{\ldots\ldots}$

(3) $\frac{4}{3}-\frac{8}{9}=\frac{\ldots\ldots-\ldots\ldots}{\ldots\ldots}=\frac{\ldots\ldots}{\ldots\ldots}$

(4) $\frac{6}{4}-\frac{5}{7}=\frac{\ldots\ldots-\ldots\ldots}{\ldots\ldots}=\frac{\ldots\ldots}{\ldots\ldots}$

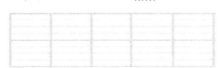

(5) $6-\frac{2}{9}=\frac{\ldots\ldots-\ldots\ldots}{\ldots\ldots}=\frac{\ldots\ldots}{\ldots\ldots}$

(6) $\frac{5}{4}-\frac{5}{7}=\frac{\ldots\ldots-\ldots\ldots}{\ldots\ldots}=\frac{\ldots\ldots}{\ldots\ldots}$

Answer Key	My Score
(1) $\frac{47}{7}$ (2) $\frac{3}{3}$ (3) $\frac{4}{9}$ (4) $\frac{22}{28}$ (5) $\frac{52}{9}$ (6) $\frac{15}{28}$	/6

LCM= Least Common Multiple

Subtraction

Name: ....

School: ....

DAY : 60

with unlike denominators

Exercise n°:1 : Multiplication review

$6\times3=\ldots$	$5\times8=\ldots$	$3\times1=\ldots$	$9\times5=\ldots$
$2\times1=\ldots$	$8\times4=\ldots$	$6\times9=\ldots$	$7\times8=\ldots$

Exercise n°:2 : Subtracting fractions

Example : $\frac{6}{5}-\frac{1}{9}=\frac{54\ -\ 5}{45}=\frac{49}{45}$ LCM(5,9) = 45

(1) $2-\frac{2}{9}=\frac{\ldots\ -\ \ldots}{\ldots}=\frac{\ldots}{\ldots}$

(2) $\frac{3}{1}-\frac{1}{8}=\frac{\ldots\ -\ \ldots}{\ldots}=\frac{\ldots}{\ldots}$

(3) $\frac{5}{4}-\frac{1}{8}=\frac{\ldots\ -\ \ldots}{\ldots}=\frac{\ldots}{\ldots}$

(4) $\frac{6}{2}-\frac{4}{7}=\frac{\ldots\ -\ \ldots}{\ldots}=\frac{\ldots}{\ldots}$

(5) $3-\frac{2}{5}=\frac{\ldots\ -\ \ldots}{\ldots}=\frac{\ldots}{\ldots}$

(6) $\frac{9}{7}-\frac{1}{2}=\frac{\ldots\ -\ \ldots}{\ldots}=\frac{\ldots}{\ldots}$

Answer Key	My Score
(1) $\frac{16}{9}$ (2) $\frac{23}{8}$ (3) $\frac{9}{8}$ (4) $\frac{34}{14}$ (5) $\frac{13}{5}$ (6) $\frac{11}{14}$	/6

*LCM= **L**east **C**ommon **M**ultiple*

Multiplication / division

Name: ....

School: ....

DAY: 61

Exercise n°:1 : Multiplication review

$4\times3=$ ...	$3\times5=$ ...	$2\times6=$ ...	$9\times1=$ ...
$4\times6=$ ...	$1\times3=$ ...	$5\times1=$ ...	$3\times7=$ ...

Exercise n°:2 Multiplying fractions

Example : $\frac{7}{2}\times\frac{1}{2}=\frac{7\times1}{2\times2}=\frac{\mathbf{7}}{\mathbf{4}}$

1. $\frac{4}{5}\times\frac{4}{5}=\frac{.....\times......}{.....\times......}=\frac{.....}{......}$

2. $\frac{2}{7}\times\frac{5}{7}=\frac{.....\times......}{.....\times......}=\frac{.....}{......}$

Exercise n°:3 Dividing fractions

Example : $\frac{3}{2}\div\frac{4}{2}=\frac{3\times2}{2\times4}=\frac{\mathbf{6}}{\mathbf{8}}$

3. $\frac{4}{7}\div\frac{2}{7}=\frac{.....\times......}{.....\times......}=\frac{.....}{......}$

4. $\frac{5}{1}\div\frac{2}{1}=\frac{.....\times......}{.....\times......}=\frac{.....}{......}$

Answer Key	My Score ☺
1. $\frac{16}{25}$ 2. $\frac{10}{49}$ 3. $\frac{28}{14}$ 4. $\frac{5}{2}$	/4

Multiplication / division

Name: ....

School: ....

DAY: 62

Exercise n°:1 : Multiplication review

$9\times3=$ ...	$5\times3=$ ...	$5\times3=$ ...	$8\times1=$ ...
$9\times4=$ ...	$1\times3=$ ...	$3\times1=$ ...	$3\times6=$ ...

Exercise n°:2 Multiplying fractions

Example : $\frac{5}{9}\times\frac{3}{9}=\frac{5\times3}{9\times9}=\frac{\mathbf{15}}{\mathbf{81}}$

1. $\frac{9}{2}\times\frac{2}{2}=\frac{\dots\times\dots}{\dots\times\dots}=\frac{\dots}{\dots}$

2. $\frac{5}{3}\times\frac{4}{3}=\frac{\dots\times\dots}{\dots\times\dots}=\frac{\dots}{\dots}$

Exercise n°:3 Dividing fractions

Example : $\frac{8}{4}\div\frac{1}{4}=\frac{8\times4}{4\times1}=\frac{\mathbf{32}}{\mathbf{4}}$

3. $\frac{9}{4}\div\frac{2}{4}=\frac{\dots\times\dots}{\dots\times\dots}=\frac{\dots}{\dots}$

4. $\frac{9}{1}\div\frac{1}{1}=\frac{\dots\times\dots}{\dots\times\dots}=\frac{\dots}{\dots}$

Answer Key	My Score
① $\frac{18}{4}$ ② $\frac{20}{9}$ ③ $\frac{36}{8}$ ④ $\frac{9}{1}$	/4

Multiplication / division

Name: ....

School: ....

DAY: 63

Exercise n°:1 : Multiplication review

$2\times8=\ldots$ $7\times9=\ldots$ $3\times7=\ldots$ $6\times1=\ldots$

$2\times4=\ldots$ $1\times8=\ldots$ $9\times8=\ldots$ $8\times1=\ldots$

Exercise n°:2 Multiplying fractions

Example : $\frac{7}{1}\times\frac{4}{1}=\frac{7\times4}{1\times1}=\frac{\mathbf{28}}{\mathbf{1}}$

1. $\frac{2}{3}\times\frac{6}{3}=\frac{\ldots\times\ldots}{\ldots\times\ldots}=\frac{\ldots}{\ldots}$

2. $\frac{9}{1}\times\frac{1}{1}=\frac{\ldots\times\ldots}{\ldots\times\ldots}=\frac{\ldots}{\ldots}$

Exercise n°:3 Dividing fractions

Example : $\frac{9}{7}\div\frac{5}{7}=\frac{9\times7}{7\times5}=\frac{\mathbf{63}}{\mathbf{35}}$

3. $\frac{6}{4}\div\frac{7}{4}=\frac{\ldots\times\ldots}{\ldots\times\ldots}=\frac{\ldots}{\ldots}$

4. $\frac{7}{8}\div\frac{6}{8}=\frac{\ldots\times\ldots}{\ldots\times\ldots}=\frac{\ldots}{\ldots}$

Answer Key	My Score
1. $\frac{12}{9}$ 2. $\frac{9}{1}$ 3. $\frac{24}{28}$ 4. $\frac{56}{48}$	/4

Multiplication / division

Name: ....

School: ....

DAY: 64

Exercise n°:1 : Multiplication review

$5 \times 4 = \dots$ $9 \times 9 = \dots$ $7 \times 2 = \dots$ $9 \times 1 = \dots$

$5 \times 3 = \dots$ $1 \times 4 = \dots$ $9 \times 4 = \dots$ $4 \times 9 = \dots$

Exercise n°:2 Multiplying fractions

Example : $\frac{5}{8} \times \frac{3}{8} = \frac{5 \times 3}{8 \times 8} = \frac{15}{64}$

1. $\frac{5}{1} \times \frac{2}{1} = \frac{\dots \times \dots}{\dots \times \dots} = \frac{\dots}{\dots}$

2. $\frac{9}{1} \times \frac{1}{1} = \frac{\dots \times \dots}{\dots \times \dots} = \frac{\dots}{\dots}$

Exercise n°:3 Dividing fractions

Example : $\frac{8}{2} \div \frac{4}{2} = \frac{8 \times 2}{2 \times 4} = \frac{16}{8}$

3. $\frac{7}{4} \div \frac{3}{4} = \frac{\dots \times \dots}{\dots \times \dots} = \frac{\dots}{\dots}$

4. $\frac{8}{3} \div \frac{3}{3} = \frac{\dots \times \dots}{\dots \times \dots} = \frac{\dots}{\dots}$

Answer Key	My Score
1. $\frac{10}{1}$ 2. $\frac{9}{1}$ 3. $\frac{28}{12}$ 4. $\frac{24}{9}$	/4

Multiplication / division

Name: ....

School: ....

DAY: 65

Exercise n°:1 : Multiplication review

$4 \times 1 =$ ...	$7 \times 3 =$ ...	$4 \times 3 =$ ...	$1 \times 1 =$ ...
$4 \times 4 =$ ...	$1 \times 1 =$ ...	$3 \times 5 =$ ...	$1 \times 6 =$ ...

Exercise n°:2 Multiplying fractions

Example : $\frac{4}{3} \times \frac{3}{3} = \frac{4 \times 3}{3 \times 3} = \frac{12}{9}$

① $\frac{4}{3} \times \frac{9}{3} = \frac{\dots \times \dots}{\dots \times \dots} = \frac{\dots}{\dots}$

② $\frac{8}{3} \times \frac{3}{3} = \frac{\dots \times \dots}{\dots \times \dots} = \frac{\dots}{\dots}$

Exercise n°:3 Dividing fractions

Example : $\frac{4}{3} \div \frac{7}{3} = \frac{4 \times 3}{3 \times 7} = \frac{12}{21}$

③ $\frac{3}{9} \div \frac{6}{9} = \frac{\dots \times \dots}{\dots \times \dots} = \frac{\dots}{\dots}$

④ $\frac{2}{8} \div \frac{3}{8} = \frac{\dots \times \dots}{\dots \times \dots} = \frac{\dots}{\dots}$

Answer Key	*My Score* ☺
① $\frac{36}{9}$ ② $\frac{24}{9}$ ③ $\frac{27}{54}$ ④ $\frac{16}{24}$	/4

Multiplication / division

Name: ....

School: ....

DAY: 66

Exercise n°:1 : Multiplication review

$9\times3=$ ...	$7\times2=$ ...	$7\times6=$ ...	$7\times1=$ ...
$9\times1=$ ...	$1\times3=$ ...	$2\times3=$ ...	$3\times5=$ ...

Exercise n°:2 Multiplying fractions

Example : $\frac{7}{4}\times\frac{3}{4}=\frac{7\times3}{4\times4}=\frac{21}{16}$

1. $\frac{9}{4}\times\frac{2}{4}=\frac{\ldots\times\ldots}{\ldots\times\ldots}=\frac{\ldots}{\ldots}$

2. $\frac{7}{7}\times\frac{3}{7}=\frac{\ldots\times\ldots}{\ldots\times\ldots}=\frac{\ldots}{\ldots}$

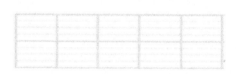

Exercise n°:3 Dividing fractions

Example : $\frac{7}{2}\div\frac{2}{2}=\frac{7\times2}{2\times2}=\frac{14}{4}$

3. $\frac{7}{6}\div\frac{2}{6}=\frac{\ldots\times\ldots}{\ldots\times\ldots}=\frac{\ldots}{\ldots}$

4. $\frac{9}{7}\div\frac{4}{7}=\frac{\ldots\times\ldots}{\ldots\times\ldots}=\frac{\ldots}{\ldots}$

Answer Key	*My Score* ☺
❶ $\frac{18}{16}$ ❷ $\frac{21}{49}$ ❸ $\frac{42}{12}$ ❹ $\frac{63}{28}$	/4

Multiplication / division

Name: ....

School: ....

DAY: 67

Exercise n°:1 : Multiplication review

$1\times5=\dots$	$1\times9=\dots$	$3\times4=\dots$	$1\times1=\dots$
$1\times1=\dots$	$1\times5=\dots$	$9\times6=\dots$	$5\times1=\dots$

Exercise n°:2 Multiplying fractions

Example : $\frac{4}{8}\times\frac{7}{8}=\frac{4\times7}{8\times8}=\frac{28}{64}$

1. $\frac{1}{9}\times\frac{3}{9}=\frac{\dots\times\dots}{\dots\times\dots}=\frac{\dots}{\dots}$

2. $\frac{8}{9}\times\frac{5}{9}=\frac{\dots\times\dots}{\dots\times\dots}=\frac{\dots}{\dots}$

Exercise n°:3 Dividing fractions

Example : $\frac{6}{8}\div\frac{8}{8}=\frac{6\times8}{8\times8}=\frac{48}{64}$

3. $\frac{3}{7}\div\frac{9}{7}=\frac{\dots\times\dots}{\dots\times\dots}=\frac{\dots}{\dots}$

4. $\frac{8}{6}\div\frac{9}{6}=\frac{\dots\times\dots}{\dots\times\dots}=\frac{\dots}{\dots}$

Answer Key	My Score ☺
1. $\frac{3}{81}$ 2. $\frac{40}{81}$ 3. $\frac{21}{63}$ 4. $\frac{48}{54}$	/4

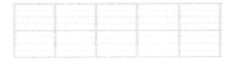

Multiplication / division

Name: ....

School: ....

DAY: 68

Exercise n°:1 : Multiplication review

$9 \times 3 =$ ...	$7 \times 7 =$ ...	$9 \times 3 =$ ...	$7 \times 1 =$ ...
$9 \times 9 =$ ...	$1 \times 3 =$ ...	$7 \times 2 =$ ...	$3 \times 9 =$ ...

Exercise n°:2 Multiplying fractions

Example : $\frac{7}{7} \times \frac{1}{7} = \frac{7 \times 1}{7 \times 7} = \frac{7}{49}$

1. $\frac{9}{4} \times \frac{4}{4} = \frac{\ldots \times \ldots}{\ldots \times \ldots} = \frac{\ldots}{\ldots}$

2. $\frac{8}{8} \times \frac{3}{8} = \frac{\ldots \times \ldots}{\ldots \times \ldots} = \frac{\ldots}{\ldots}$

Exercise n°:3 Dividing fractions

Example : $\frac{6}{1} \div \frac{4}{1} = \frac{6 \times 1}{1 \times 4} = \frac{6}{4}$

3. $\frac{6}{8} \div \frac{3}{8} = \frac{\ldots \times \ldots}{\ldots \times \ldots} = \frac{\ldots}{\ldots}$

4. $\frac{5}{2} \div \frac{4}{2} = \frac{\ldots \times \ldots}{\ldots \times \ldots} = \frac{\ldots}{\ldots}$

Answer Key	My Score
1. $\frac{36}{16}$ 2. $\frac{24}{64}$ 3. $\frac{48}{24}$ 4. $\frac{10}{8}$	/4

Multiplication / division

Name: ……………………

School: ……………………

DAY: 69

Exercise n°:1 : Multiplication review

$8\times4=\ldots$	$7\times2=\ldots$	$1\times3=\ldots$	$1\times1=\ldots$
$8\times6=\ldots$	$1\times4=\ldots$	$5\times3=\ldots$	$4\times6=\ldots$

Exercise n°:2 Multiplying fractions

Example : $\frac{6}{4}\times\frac{6}{1}=\frac{6\times6}{4\times1}=\frac{\mathbf{36}}{\mathbf{4}}$

1. $\frac{8}{3}\times\frac{2}{3}=\frac{\ldots\times\ldots}{\ldots\times\ldots}=\frac{\ldots}{\ldots}$

2. $\frac{1}{1}\times\frac{9}{2}=\frac{\ldots\times\ldots}{\ldots\times\ldots}=\frac{\ldots}{\ldots}$

Exercise n°:3 Dividing fractions

Example : $\frac{7}{7}\div\frac{3}{2}=\frac{7\times2}{7\times3}=\frac{\mathbf{14}}{\mathbf{21}}$

3. $\frac{9}{4}\div\frac{4}{5}=\frac{\ldots\times\ldots}{\ldots\times\ldots}=\frac{\ldots}{\ldots}$

4. $\frac{1}{9}\div\frac{3}{5}=\frac{\ldots\times\ldots}{\ldots\times\ldots}=\frac{\ldots}{\ldots}$

Answer Key	My Score ☺
1. $\frac{16}{9}$ 2. $\frac{9}{2}$ 3. $\frac{45}{16}$ 4. $\frac{5}{27}$	/4

Multiplication / division

Name: ....

School: ....

DAY: 70

Exercise n°:1 : Multiplication review

$5\times2=$ ...	$7\times7=$ ...	$6\times3=$ ...	$5\times2=$ ...
$5\times8=$ ...	$1\times2=$ ...	$4\times5=$ ...	$2\times8=$ ...

Exercise n°:2 Multiplying fractions

Example : $\frac{9}{2}\times\frac{2}{8}=\frac{9\times2}{2\times8}=\frac{\mathbf{18}}{\mathbf{16}}$

1. $\frac{5}{4}\times\frac{1}{8}=\frac{\dots\times\dots}{\dots\times\dots}=\frac{\dots}{\dots}$

2. $\frac{7}{2}\times\frac{4}{5}=\frac{\dots\times\dots}{\dots\times\dots}=\frac{\dots}{\dots}$

Exercise n°:3 Dividing fractions

Example : $\frac{9}{2}\div\frac{1}{6}=\frac{9\times6}{2\times1}=\frac{\mathbf{54}}{\mathbf{2}}$

3. $\frac{5}{1}\div\frac{4}{7}=\frac{\dots\times\dots}{\dots\times\dots}=\frac{\dots}{\dots}$

4. $\frac{5}{1}\div\frac{3}{7}=\frac{\dots\times\dots}{\dots\times\dots}=\frac{\dots}{\dots}$

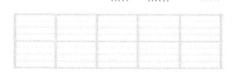

Answer Key	*My Score* ☺
1. $\frac{5}{32}$ 2. $\frac{28}{10}$ 3. $\frac{35}{4}$ 4. $\frac{35}{3}$	/4

Multiplication / division

Name: ....

School: ....

DAY: 71

Exercise n°:1 : Multiplication review

$1\times6=$ ...	$9\times9=$ ...	$2\times3=$ ...	$8\times1=$ ...
$1\times4=$ ...	$1\times6=$ ...	$1\times8=$ ...	$6\times7=$ ...

Exercise n°:2 Multiplying fractions

Example : $\frac{4}{4}\times\frac{1}{3}=\frac{4\times1}{4\times3}=\frac{4}{12}$

1 $\frac{1}{3}\times\frac{5}{1}=\frac{\dots\times\dots}{\dots\times\dots}=\frac{\dots}{\dots}$

2 $\frac{3}{5}\times\frac{5}{8}=\frac{\dots\times\dots}{\dots\times\dots}=\frac{\dots}{\dots}$

Exercise n°:3 Dividing fractions

Example : $\frac{1}{2}\div\frac{3}{9}=\frac{1\times9}{2\times3}=\frac{9}{6}$

3 $\frac{9}{8}\div\frac{8}{2}=\frac{\dots\times\dots}{\dots\times\dots}=\frac{\dots}{\dots}$

4 $\frac{5}{5}\div\frac{3}{4}=\frac{\dots\times\dots}{\dots\times\dots}=\frac{\dots}{\dots}$

Answer Key	My Score ☺
1 $\frac{5}{3}$ **2** $\frac{15}{40}$ **3** $\frac{18}{64}$ **4** $\frac{20}{15}$	/4

Multiplication / division

Name: ....

School: ....

DAY: 72

Exercise n°:1 : Multiplication review

$9\times5=$ ...	$7\times5=$ ...	$9\times2=$ ...	$6\times7=$ ...
$9\times9=$ ...	$2\times5=$ ...	$3\times3=$ ...	$5\times5=$ ...

Exercise n°:2 Multiplying fractions

Example : $\frac{5}{2}\times\frac{4}{7}=\frac{5\times4}{2\times7}=\frac{20}{14}$

1. $\frac{9}{3}\times\frac{3}{7}=\frac{\dots\times\dots}{\dots\times\dots}=\frac{\dots}{\dots}$

2. $\frac{5}{4}\times\frac{5}{6}=\frac{\dots\times\dots}{\dots\times\dots}=\frac{\dots}{\dots}$

Exercise n°:3 Dividing fractions

Example : $\frac{5}{4}\div\frac{3}{7}=\frac{5\times7}{4\times3}=\frac{35}{12}$

3. $\frac{7}{4}\div\frac{3}{9}=\frac{\dots\times\dots}{\dots\times\dots}=\frac{\dots}{\dots}$

4. $\frac{8}{2}\div\frac{2}{8}=\frac{\dots\times\dots}{\dots\times\dots}=\frac{\dots}{\dots}$

Answer Key	My Score
1. $\frac{27}{21}$ 2. $\frac{25}{24}$ 3. $\frac{63}{12}$ 4. $\frac{64}{4}$	/4

Multiplication / division

Name: ....

School: ....

DAY: 73

Exercise n°:1 : Multiplication review

$9\times2=\ldots$	$6\times8=\ldots$	$1\times8=\ldots$	$9\times7=\ldots$
$9\times5=\ldots$	$8\times2=\ldots$	$1\times4=\ldots$	$2\times4=\ldots$

Exercise n°:2 Multiplying fractions

Example : $\frac{2}{8}\times\frac{2}{6}=\frac{2\times2}{8\times6}=\frac{4}{48}$

1. $\frac{9}{7}\times\frac{6}{6}=\frac{\ldots\times\ldots}{\ldots\times\ldots}=\frac{\ldots}{\ldots}$

2. $\frac{3}{4}\times\frac{6}{6}=\frac{\ldots\times\ldots}{\ldots\times\ldots}=\frac{\ldots}{\ldots}$

Exercise n°:3 Dividing fractions

Example : $\frac{3}{5}\div\frac{5}{1}=\frac{3\times1}{5\times5}=\frac{3}{25}$

3. $\frac{5}{5}\div\frac{9}{1}=\frac{\ldots\times\ldots}{\ldots\times\ldots}=\frac{\ldots}{\ldots}$

4. $\frac{8}{4}\div\frac{6}{1}=\frac{\ldots\times\ldots}{\ldots\times\ldots}=\frac{\ldots}{\ldots}$

Answer Key	My Score
1. $\frac{54}{42}$ 2. $\frac{18}{24}$ 3. $\frac{5}{45}$ 4. $\frac{8}{24}$	/4

Multiplication / division

Name: ....

School: ....

DAY: 74

Exercise n°:1 : Multiplication review

$7\times1=$ ...	$6\times9=$ ...	$7\times4=$ ...	$7\times2=$ ...
$7\times7=$ ...	$1\times1=$ ...	$3\times5=$ ...	$1\times7=$ ...

Exercise n°:2 Multiplying fractions

Example : $\frac{6}{4}\times\frac{3}{8}=\frac{6\times3}{4\times8}=\frac{\mathbf{18}}{\mathbf{32}}$

1. $\frac{7}{1}\times\frac{5}{7}=\frac{\dots\times\dots}{\dots\times\dots}=\frac{\dots}{\dots}$

2. $\frac{5}{2}\times\frac{3}{9}=\frac{\dots\times\dots}{\dots\times\dots}=\frac{\dots}{\dots}$

Exercise n°:3 Dividing fractions

Example : $\frac{8}{1}\div\frac{1}{8}=\frac{8\times8}{1\times1}=\frac{\mathbf{64}}{\mathbf{1}}$

3. $\frac{9}{1}\div\frac{2}{8}=\frac{\dots\times\dots}{\dots\times\dots}=\frac{\dots}{\dots}$

4. $\frac{7}{2}\div\frac{3}{6}=\frac{\dots\times\dots}{\dots\times\dots}=\frac{\dots}{\dots}$

Answer Key	*My Score* ☺
1. $\frac{35}{7}$ 2. $\frac{15}{18}$ 3. $\frac{72}{2}$ 4. $\frac{42}{6}$	/4

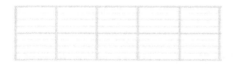

Multiplication / division

Name: ....

School: ....

DAY: 75

Exercise n°:1 : Multiplication review

$3\times7=\dots$	$6\times2=\dots$	$7\times2=\dots$	$4\times5=\dots$
$3\times3=\dots$	$2\times7=\dots$	$2\times7=\dots$	$7\times1=\dots$

Exercise n°:2 Multiplying fractions

Example : $\frac{5}{3}\times\frac{4}{2}=\frac{5\times4}{3\times2}=\frac{20}{6}$

1. $\frac{3}{6}\times\frac{7}{7}=\frac{\dots\times\dots}{\dots\times\dots}=\frac{\dots}{\dots}$

2. $\frac{5}{2}\times\frac{1}{2}=\frac{\dots\times\dots}{\dots\times\dots}=\frac{\dots}{\dots}$

Exercise n°:3 Dividing fractions

Example : $\frac{1}{1}\div\frac{9}{6}=\frac{1\times6}{1\times9}=\frac{6}{9}$

3. $\frac{1}{6}\div\frac{3}{7}=\frac{\dots\times\dots}{\dots\times\dots}=\frac{\dots}{\dots}$

4. $\frac{5}{9}\div\frac{5}{1}=\frac{\dots\times\dots}{\dots\times\dots}=\frac{\dots}{\dots}$

Answer Key	My Score
1. $\frac{21}{42}$ 2. $\frac{5}{4}$ 3. $\frac{7}{18}$ 4. $\frac{5}{45}$	/4

Multiplication / division

Name: ....

School: ....

DAY: 76

Exercise n°:1 : Multiplication review

$8\times5=\ldots$	$9\times8=\ldots$	$6\times4=\ldots$	$5\times3=\ldots$
$8\times8=\ldots$	$2\times5=\ldots$	$4\times1=\ldots$	$5\times5=\ldots$

Exercise n°:2 Multiplying fractions

Example : $\frac{7}{2}\times\frac{2}{5}=\frac{7\times2}{2\times5}=\frac{14}{10}$

1. $\frac{8}{2}\times\frac{5}{8}=\frac{\ldots\times\ldots}{\ldots\times\ldots}=\frac{\ldots}{\ldots}$

2. $\frac{8}{3}\times\frac{3}{5}=\frac{\ldots\times\ldots}{\ldots\times\ldots}=\frac{\ldots}{\ldots}$

Exercise n°:3 Dividing fractions

Example : $\frac{5}{4}\div\frac{3}{9}=\frac{5\times9}{4\times3}=\frac{45}{12}$

3. $\frac{5}{4}\div\frac{1}{5}=\frac{\ldots\times\ldots}{\ldots\times\ldots}=\frac{\ldots}{\ldots}$

4. $\frac{5}{2}\div\frac{3}{8}=\frac{\ldots\times\ldots}{\ldots\times\ldots}=\frac{\ldots}{\ldots}$

Answer Key	My Score
1. $\frac{40}{16}$ 2. $\frac{24}{15}$ 3. $\frac{25}{4}$ 4. $\frac{40}{6}$	/4

Multiplication / division

Name: ....

School: ....

DAY: 77

Exercise n°:1 : Multiplication review

$2\times7=\ldots$	$8\times5=\ldots$	$3\times9=\ldots$	$9\times5=\ldots$
$2\times8=\ldots$	$9\times7=\ldots$	$3\times9=\ldots$	$7\times5=\ldots$

Exercise n°:2 Multiplying fractions

Example : $\frac{3}{7}\times\frac{1}{1}=\frac{3\times1}{7\times1}=\frac{3}{7}$

1 $\frac{2}{4}\times\frac{6}{7}=\frac{\ldots\times\ldots}{\ldots\times\ldots}=\frac{\ldots}{\ldots}$

2 $\frac{7}{7}\times\frac{9}{1}=\frac{\ldots\times\ldots}{\ldots\times\ldots}=\frac{\ldots}{\ldots}$

Exercise n°:3 Dividing fractions

Example : $\frac{6}{9}\div\frac{3}{4}=\frac{6\times4}{9\times3}=\frac{24}{27}$

3 $\frac{6}{6}\div\frac{4}{7}=\frac{\ldots\times\ldots}{\ldots\times\ldots}=\frac{\ldots}{\ldots}$

4 $\frac{9}{9}\div\frac{7}{4}=\frac{\ldots\times\ldots}{\ldots\times\ldots}=\frac{\ldots}{\ldots}$

Answer Key	My Score ☺
1 $\frac{12}{28}$ **2** $\frac{63}{7}$ **3** $\frac{42}{24}$ **4** $\frac{36}{63}$	/4

Multiplication / division

Name: ....

School: ....

DAY: 78

Exercise n°:1 : Multiplication review

$9\times3=\ldots$	$9\times8=\ldots$	$5\times1=\ldots$	$5\times9=\ldots$
$9\times8=\ldots$	$1\times3=\ldots$	$3\times3=\ldots$	$3\times8=\ldots$

Exercise n°:2 Multiplying fractions

Example : $\frac{7}{3}\times\frac{2}{7}=\frac{7\times2}{3\times7}=\frac{\mathbf{14}}{\mathbf{21}}$

1. $\frac{9}{3}\times\frac{4}{8}=\frac{\ldots\times\ldots}{\ldots\times\ldots}=\frac{\ldots}{\ldots}$

2. $\frac{7}{1}\times\frac{5}{6}=\frac{\ldots\times\ldots}{\ldots\times\ldots}=\frac{\ldots}{\ldots}$

Exercise n°:3 Dividing fractions

Example : $\frac{8}{3}\div\frac{5}{6}=\frac{8\times6}{3\times5}=\frac{\mathbf{48}}{\mathbf{15}}$

3. $\frac{5}{4}\div\frac{3}{7}=\frac{\ldots\times\ldots}{\ldots\times\ldots}=\frac{\ldots}{\ldots}$

4. $\frac{5}{1}\div\frac{3}{9}=\frac{\ldots\times\ldots}{\ldots\times\ldots}=\frac{\ldots}{\ldots}$

Answer Key	My Score ☺
1 $\frac{36}{24}$ **2** $\frac{35}{6}$ **3** $\frac{35}{12}$ **4** $\frac{45}{3}$	/4

Multiplication / division

Name: ....

School: ....

DAY : 79

Exercise n°:1 : Multiplication review

$2\times8=\ldots$	$3\times2=\ldots$	$2\times3=\ldots$	$4\times7=\ldots$
$2\times9=\ldots$	$3\times8=\ldots$	$8\times6=\ldots$	$8\times4=\ldots$

Exercise n°:2 Multiplying fractions

Example : $\frac{3}{1}\times\frac{9}{9}=\frac{3\times9}{1\times9}=\frac{27}{9}$

1 $\frac{2}{7}\times\frac{1}{2}=\frac{\ldots\times\ldots}{\ldots\times\ldots}=\frac{\ldots}{\ldots}$

2 $\frac{3}{4}\times\frac{7}{7}=\frac{\ldots\times\ldots}{\ldots\times\ldots}=\frac{\ldots}{\ldots}$

Exercise n°:3 Dividing fractions

Example : $\frac{7}{7}\div\frac{9}{8}=\frac{7\times8}{7\times9}=\frac{56}{63}$

3 $\frac{4}{1}\div\frac{2}{6}=\frac{\ldots\times\ldots}{\ldots\times\ldots}=\frac{\ldots}{\ldots}$

4 $\frac{7}{1}\div\frac{9}{5}=\frac{\ldots\times\ldots}{\ldots\times\ldots}=\frac{\ldots}{\ldots}$

Answer Key	My Score
1 $\frac{2}{14}$ **2** $\frac{21}{28}$ **3** $\frac{24}{2}$ **4** $\frac{35}{9}$	/4

Multiplication / division

Name: ....

School: ....

DAY: 80

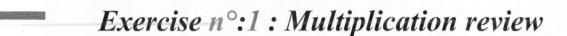

Exercise n°:1 : Multiplication review

$7\times1=$ ...	$7\times8=$ ...	$6\times1=$ ...	$9\times8=$ ...
$7\times5=$ ...	$1\times1=$ ...	$4\times1=$ ...	$1\times7=$ ...

Exercise n°:2 Multiplying fractions

Example : $\frac{7}{4}\times\frac{5}{7}=\frac{7\times5}{4\times7}=\frac{35}{28}$

1. $\frac{7}{4}\times\frac{3}{8}=\frac{\dots\times\dots}{\dots\times\dots}=\frac{\dots}{\dots}$

2. $\frac{5}{2}\times\frac{5}{8}=\frac{\dots\times\dots}{\dots\times\dots}=\frac{\dots}{\dots}$

Exercise n°:3 Dividing fractions

Example : $\frac{9}{3}\div\frac{5}{9}=\frac{9\times9}{3\times5}=\frac{81}{15}$

3. $\frac{7}{4}\div\frac{5}{8}=\frac{\dots\times\dots}{\dots\times\dots}=\frac{\dots}{\dots}$

4. $\frac{9}{2}\div\frac{1}{5}=\frac{\dots\times\dots}{\dots\times\dots}=\frac{\dots}{\dots}$

Answer Key	My Score
1. $\frac{21}{32}$ 2. $\frac{25}{16}$ 3. $\frac{56}{20}$ 4. $\frac{45}{2}$	/4

Equivalent

Name: ....

School: ....

DAY: 81

1) Find the equivalent fractions

Example: $\frac{3}{4} = \frac{....?}{16} = \frac{12}{16}$ (×4)

(E_1) $\frac{1}{9} = \frac{......}{54}$

(E_2) $\frac{6}{5} = \frac{18}{......}$

(E_3) $\frac{6}{......} = \frac{30}{25}$

(E_4) $\frac{......}{9} = \frac{63}{81}$

(E_5) $\frac{......}{8} = \frac{72}{72}$

(E_6) $\frac{2}{1} = \frac{......}{2}$

(E_7) $\frac{1}{3} = \frac{7}{......}$

(E_8) $\frac{......}{6} = \frac{5}{6}$

(E_9) $\frac{9}{3} = \frac{......}{15}$

(E_{10}) $\frac{2}{2} = \frac{14}{......}$

(E_{11}) $\frac{......}{8} = \frac{6}{24}$

(E_{12}) $\frac{6}{5} = \frac{......}{25}$

(E_{13}) $\frac{2}{2} = \frac{6}{......}$

(E_{14}) $\frac{1}{......} = \frac{3}{3}$

(E_{15}) $\frac{......}{1} = \frac{40}{5}$

Answer Key	My Score
(E_1) = 6 (E_2)=15 (E_3) = 5 (E_4)=7 (E_5)=8 (E_6) = 4 (E_7)=21 (E_8)=5 (E_9)=45 (E_{10})=14 (E_{11})=2 (E_{12})=30 (E_{13})=6 (E_{14})=1 (E_{15})=8	/15

Equivalent

Name: ....

School: ....

DAY: 82

1) Find the equivalent fractions

Example: $\frac{6}{8} = \frac{\ldots?}{56} = \frac{42}{56}$ ($\times 7$ numerator, $\times 7$ denominator)

(E_1) $\frac{9}{4} = \frac{\ldots\ldots}{8}$	(E_2) $\frac{2}{3} = \frac{18}{\ldots\ldots}$	(E_3) $\frac{6}{\ldots\ldots} = \frac{42}{42}$
(E_4) $\frac{\ldots\ldots}{1} = \frac{48}{6}$	(E_5) $\frac{\ldots\ldots}{6} = \frac{24}{48}$	(E_6) $\frac{1}{9} = \frac{\ldots\ldots}{54}$
(E_7) $\frac{7}{8} = \frac{21}{\ldots\ldots}$	(E_8) $\frac{\ldots\ldots}{2} = \frac{1}{2}$	(E_9) $\frac{8}{2} = \frac{\ldots\ldots}{18}$
(E_{10}) $\frac{5}{8} = \frac{35}{\ldots\ldots}$	(E_{11}) $\frac{\ldots\ldots}{4} = \frac{80}{40}$	(E_{12}) $\frac{2}{5} = \frac{\ldots\ldots}{5}$
(E_{13}) $\frac{5}{1} = \frac{10}{\ldots\ldots}$	(E_{14}) $\frac{9}{\ldots\ldots} = \frac{9}{4}$	(E_{15}) $\frac{\ldots\ldots}{2} = \frac{45}{18}$

Answer Key	My Score
$(E_1) = 18$ $(E_2)=27$ $(E_3)=6$ $(E_4)=8$ $(E_5)=3$ $(E_6) = 6$ $(E_7)=24$ $(E_8)=1$ $(E_9)=72$ $(E_{10})=56$ $(E_{11})=8$ $(E_{12})=2$ $(E_{13})=2$ $(E_{14})=4$ $(E_{15})=5$	/15

Equivalent

Name: ....

School: ....

DAY: 83

1) Find the equivalent fractions

Example: $\frac{2}{2} = \frac{....?}{10} = \frac{10}{10}$ (×5 on numerator and denominator)

(E_1) $\frac{7}{9} = \frac{......}{9}$

(E_2) $\frac{6}{9} = \frac{18}{......}$

(E_3) $\frac{2}{......} = \frac{20}{10}$

(E_4) $\frac{......}{5} = \frac{32}{20}$

(E_5) $\frac{......}{6} = \frac{36}{36}$

(E_6) $\frac{4}{2} = \frac{......}{16}$

(E_7) $\frac{9}{7} = \frac{18}{......}$

(E_8) $\frac{......}{8} = \frac{4}{16}$

(E_9) $\frac{9}{6} = \frac{......}{12}$

(E_{10}) $\frac{7}{5} = \frac{56}{......}$

(E_{11}) $\frac{......}{7} = \frac{4}{14}$

(E_{12}) $\frac{5}{7} = \frac{......}{28}$

(E_{13}) $\frac{4}{9} = \frac{4}{......}$

(E_{14}) $\frac{9}{......} = \frac{27}{12}$

(E_{15}) $\frac{......}{7} = \frac{18}{14}$

Answer Key	My Score
(E_1) = 7, (E_2)=27, (E_3) = 1, (E_4)=8, (E_5)=6 (E_6) = 32, (E_7)=14, (E_8)=2, (E_9)=18, (E_{10})=40 (E_{11})=2, (E_{12})=20, (E_{13})=9, (E_{14})=4, (E_{15})=9	/15

Equivalent

Name: ....

School: ....

DAY: 84

1) Find the equivalent fractions

Example: $\frac{5}{7} = \frac{\dots?}{21} = \frac{15}{21}$ (×3 on top and bottom)

(E_1) $\frac{3}{1} = \frac{\dots\dots}{1}$

(E_2) $\frac{9}{2} = \frac{63}{\dots\dots}$

(E_3) $\frac{9}{\dots\dots} = \frac{9}{3}$

(E_4) $\frac{\dots\dots}{9} = \frac{10}{45}$

(E_5) $\frac{\dots\dots}{5} = \frac{50}{50}$

(E_6) $\frac{2}{2} = \frac{\dots\dots}{18}$

(E_7) $\frac{1}{5} = \frac{8}{\dots\dots}$

(E_8) $\frac{\dots\dots}{2} = \frac{20}{20}$

(E_9) $\frac{6}{5} = \frac{\dots\dots}{30}$

(E_{10}) $\frac{1}{4} = \frac{6}{\dots\dots}$

(E_{11}) $\frac{\dots\dots}{4} = \frac{2}{4}$

(E_{12}) $\frac{8}{4} = \frac{\dots\dots}{8}$

(E_{13}) $\frac{7}{3} = \frac{14}{\dots\dots}$

(E_{14}) $\frac{2}{\dots\dots} = \frac{2}{7}$

(E_{15}) $\frac{\dots\dots}{5} = \frac{10}{10}$

Answer Key	My Score
(E_1) = 3 (E_2)=14 (E_3) = 3 (E_4)=2 (E_5)=5 (E_6) = 18 (E_7)=40 (E_8)=2 (E_9)=36 (E_{10})=24 (E_{11})=2 (E_{12})=16 (E_{13})=6 (E_{14})=7 (E_{15})=5	/15

Equivalent

Name: ....

School: ....

DAY: 85

1) Find the equivalent fractions

Example: $\frac{3}{9} = \frac{....?}{81} = \frac{27}{81}$ (numerator and denominator × 9)

(E_1) $\frac{7}{6} = \frac{......}{6}$

(E_2) $\frac{8}{9} = \frac{40}{......}$

(E_3) $\frac{4}{......} = \frac{12}{27}$

(E_4) $\frac{......}{5} = \frac{21}{35}$

(E_5) $\frac{......}{7} = \frac{81}{63}$

(E_6) $\frac{6}{5} = \frac{......}{45}$

(E_7) $\frac{6}{8} = \frac{30}{......}$

(E_8) $\frac{......}{1} = \frac{5}{1}$

(E_9) $\frac{7}{6} = \frac{......}{42}$

(E_{10}) $\frac{4}{9} = \frac{4}{......}$

(E_{11}) $\frac{......}{1} = \frac{36}{9}$

(E_{12}) $\frac{7}{3} = \frac{......}{6}$

(E_{13}) $\frac{2}{9} = \frac{6}{......}$

(E_{14}) $\frac{5}{......} = \frac{35}{49}$

(E_{15}) $\frac{......}{9} = \frac{3}{9}$

Answer Key	My Score
(E_1) = 7 (E_2)=45 (E_3) = 9 (E_4)=3 (E_5)=9 (E_6) = 54 (E_7)=40 (E_8)=5 (E_9)=49 (E_{10})=9 (E_{11})=4 (E_{12})=14 (E_{13})=27 (E_{14})=7 (E_{15})=3	/15

Equivalent

Name: ....

School: ....

DAY: 86

1) Find the equivalent fractions

Example: $\frac{7}{5} = \frac{....?}{10} = \frac{14}{10}$ (×2 on the numerator, ×2 on the denominator)

$(E_1)\ \frac{4}{2} = \frac{......}{4}$ $(E_2)\ \frac{2}{9} = \frac{6}{......}$ $(E_3)\ \frac{1}{......} = \frac{9}{81}$

$(E_4)\ \frac{......}{8} = \frac{8}{16}$ $(E_5)\ \frac{......}{8} = \frac{6}{48}$ $(E_6)\ \frac{3}{4} = \frac{......}{12}$

$(E_7)\ \frac{6}{2} = \frac{54}{......}$ $(E_8)\ \frac{......}{2} = \frac{45}{10}$ $(E_9)\ \frac{9}{7} = \frac{......}{14}$

$(E_{10})\ \frac{8}{2} = \frac{16}{......}$ $(E_{11})\ \frac{......}{6} = \frac{4}{6}$ $(E_{12})\ \frac{6}{3} = \frac{......}{18}$

$(E_{13})\ \frac{2}{4} = \frac{16}{......}$ $(E_{14})\ \frac{2}{......} = \frac{8}{20}$ $(E_{15})\ \frac{......}{2} = \frac{36}{8}$

Answer Key	My Score
$(E_1) = 8$ $(E_2)=27$ $(E_3) = 9$ $(E_4)=4$ $(E_5)=1$ $(E_6) = 9$ $(E_7)=18$ $(E_8)=9$ $(E_9)=18$ $(E_{10})=4$ $(E_{11})=4$ $(E_{12})=36$ $(E_{13})=32$ $(E_{14})=5$ $(E_{15})=9$	/15

Equivalent

Name: ....

School: ....

DAY: 87

1) Find the equivalent fractions

Example: $\frac{3}{2} = \frac{\ldots ?}{10} = \frac{15}{10}$ (×5 on the numerator, ×5 on the denominator)

(E_1) $\frac{5}{5} = \frac{\ldots\ldots}{20}$ (E_2) $\frac{9}{7} = \frac{81}{\ldots\ldots}$ (E_3) $\frac{1}{\ldots\ldots} = \frac{4}{32}$

(E_4) $\frac{\ldots\ldots}{8} = \frac{15}{40}$ (E_5) $\frac{\ldots\ldots}{1} = \frac{21}{7}$ (E_6) $\frac{8}{5} = \frac{\ldots\ldots}{45}$

(E_7) $\frac{6}{2} = \frac{24}{\ldots\ldots}$ (E_8) $\frac{\ldots\ldots}{8} = \frac{8}{64}$ (E_9) $\frac{5}{7} = \frac{\ldots\ldots}{56}$

(E_{10}) $\frac{5}{6} = \frac{20}{\ldots\ldots}$ (E_{11}) $\frac{\ldots\ldots}{6} = \frac{24}{36}$ (E_{12}) $\frac{4}{6} = \frac{\ldots\ldots}{6}$

(E_{13}) $\frac{5}{1} = \frac{50}{\ldots\ldots}$ (E_{14}) $\frac{1}{\ldots\ldots} = \frac{3}{12}$ (E_{15}) $\frac{\ldots\ldots}{8} = \frac{24}{64}$

Answer Key	My Score
$(E_1) = 20$ $(E_2)=63$ $(E_3) = 8$ $(E_4)=3$ $(E_5)=3$ $(E_6) = 72$ $(E_7)=8$ $(E_8)=1$ $(E_9)=40$ $(E_{10})=24$ $(E_{11})=4$ $(E_{12})=4$ $(E_{13})=10$ $(E_{14})=4$ $(E_{15})=3$	/15

Equivalent

Name: ....

School: ....

DAY: 88

1) Find the equivalent fractions

Example: $\frac{2}{5} = \frac{....?}{40} = \frac{16}{40}$ (×8 on the top and ×8 on the bottom)

(E_1) $\frac{3}{7} = \frac{......}{14}$ (E_2) $\frac{7}{7} = \frac{42}{......}$ (E_3) $\frac{5}{......} = \frac{35}{14}$

(E_4) $\frac{......}{9} = \frac{60}{90}$ (E_5) $\frac{......}{9} = \frac{16}{36}$ (E_6) $\frac{1}{2} = \frac{......}{16}$

(E_7) $\frac{7}{1} = \frac{49}{......}$ (E_8) $\frac{......}{3} = \frac{81}{27}$ (E_9) $\frac{9}{9} = \frac{......}{27}$

(E_{10}) $\frac{1}{4} = \frac{7}{......}$ (E_{11}) $\frac{......}{1} = \frac{30}{5}$ (E_{12}) $\frac{8}{5} = \frac{......}{10}$

(E_{13}) $\frac{6}{3} = \frac{30}{......}$ (E_{14}) $\frac{1}{......} = \frac{4}{36}$ (E_{15}) $\frac{......}{1} = \frac{35}{5}$

Answer Key	My Score
$(E_1) = 6$ $(E_2)=42$ $(E_3) = 2$ $(E_4)=6$ $(E_5)=4$ $(E_6) = 8$ $(E_7)=7$ $(E_8)=9$ $(E_9)=27$ $(E_{10})=28$ $(E_{11})=6$ $(E_{12})=16$ $(E_{13})=15$ $(E_{14})=9$ $(E_{15})=7$	/15

Equivalent

Name: ....

School: ....

DAY: 89

1) Find the equivalent fractions

Example: $\frac{8}{1} = \frac{\ldots?}{6} = \frac{48}{6}$ ($\times 6$ numerator, $\times 6$ denominator)

(E1) $\frac{2}{5} = \frac{\ldots\ldots}{45}$ (E2) $\frac{2}{4} = \frac{12}{\ldots\ldots}$ (E3) $\frac{9}{\ldots\ldots} = \frac{72}{48}$

(E4) $\frac{\ldots\ldots}{1} = \frac{30}{6}$ (E5) $\frac{\ldots\ldots}{8} = \frac{64}{64}$ (E6) $\frac{6}{4} = \frac{\ldots\ldots}{40}$

(E7) $\frac{9}{5} = \frac{81}{\ldots\ldots}$ (E8) $\frac{\ldots\ldots}{8} = \frac{25}{40}$ (E9) $\frac{7}{2} = \frac{\ldots\ldots}{6}$

(E10) $\frac{6}{1} = \frac{6}{\ldots\ldots}$ (E11) $\frac{\ldots\ldots}{2} = \frac{25}{10}$ (E12) $\frac{2}{2} = \frac{\ldots\ldots}{6}$

(E13) $\frac{7}{9} = \frac{35}{\ldots\ldots}$ (E14) $\frac{1}{\ldots\ldots} = \frac{1}{7}$ (E15) $\frac{\ldots\ldots}{7} = \frac{20}{70}$

Answer Key	My Score
(E1) = 18 (E2)=24 (E3) = 6 (E4)=5 (E5)=8 (E6) = 60 (E7)=45 (E8)=5 (E9)=21 (E10)=1 (E11)=5 (E12)=6 (E13)=45 (E14)=7 (E15)=2	/15

Equivalent

Name: ....

School: ....

DAY: 90

1) Find the equivalent fractions

Example: $\frac{6}{1} = \frac{....?}{9} = \frac{54}{9}$ (×9 numerator, ×9 denominator)

(E_1) $\frac{4}{7} = \frac{......}{70}$

(E_2) $\frac{2}{6} = \frac{12}{......}$

(E_3) $\frac{3}{......} = \frac{21}{42}$

(E_4) $\frac{......}{3} = \frac{12}{6}$

(E_5) $\frac{......}{9} = \frac{30}{45}$

(E_6) $\frac{1}{1} = \frac{......}{9}$

(E_7) $\frac{5}{6} = \frac{20}{......}$

(E_8) $\frac{......}{7} = \frac{21}{49}$

(E_9) $\frac{5}{5} = \frac{......}{50}$

(E_{10}) $\frac{4}{7} = \frac{8}{......}$

(E_{11}) $\frac{......}{7} = \frac{15}{21}$

(E_{12}) $\frac{8}{7} = \frac{......}{70}$

(E_{13}) $\frac{3}{6} = \frac{15}{......}$

(E_{14}) $\frac{7}{......} = \frac{70}{80}$

(E_{15}) $\frac{......}{4} = \frac{9}{36}$

Answer Key	My Score
$(E_1) = 40$ $(E_2)=36$ $(E_3)= 6$ $(E_4)=6$ $(E_5)=6$ $(E_6) = 9$ $(E_7)=24$ $(E_8)=3$ $(E_9)=50$ $(E_{10})=14$ $(E_{11})=5$ $(E_{12})=80$ $(E_{13})=30$ $(E_{14})=8$ $(E_{15})=1$	/15

Equivalent

Name: ....

School: ....

DAY: 91

1) Find the equivalent fractions

Example: $\frac{1}{4} = \frac{....?}{24} = \frac{6}{24}$ (×6)

$(E_1)\ \frac{4}{8} = \frac{......}{64}$ $(E_2)\ \frac{6}{5} = \frac{30}{......}$ $(E_3)\ \frac{5}{......} = \frac{40}{16}$

$(E_4)\ \frac{......}{5} = \frac{18}{15}$ $(E_5)\ \frac{......}{4} = \frac{10}{20}$ $(E_6)\ \frac{8}{8} = \frac{......}{64}$

$(E_7)\ \frac{3}{4} = \frac{15}{......}$ $(E_8)\ \frac{......}{2} = \frac{64}{16}$ $(E_9)\ \frac{6}{7} = \frac{......}{35}$

$(E_{10})\ \frac{1}{2} = \frac{4}{......}$ $(E_{11})\ \frac{......}{5} = \frac{32}{40}$ $(E_{12})\ \frac{3}{8} = \frac{......}{48}$

$(E_{13})\ \frac{8}{3} = \frac{32}{......}$ $(E_{14})\ \frac{9}{......} = \frac{72}{16}$ $(E_{15})\ \frac{......}{7} = \frac{24}{21}$

Answer Key	My Score
$(E_1) = 32$ $(E_2)=25$ $(E_3) = 2$ $(E_4)=6$ $(E_5)=2$ $(E_6) = 64$ $(E_7)=20$ $(E_8)=8$ $(E_9)=30$ $(E_{10})=8$ $(E_{11})=4$ $(E_{12})=18$ $(E_{13})=12$ $(E_{14})=2$ $(E_{15})=8$	/15

Equivalent

Name: ....

School: ....

DAY: 92

1) Find the equivalent fractions

Example: $\frac{3}{1} = \frac{....?}{1} = \frac{3}{1}$ ($\times 1$, $\times 1$)

(E_1) $\frac{4}{1} = \frac{......}{2}$

(E_2) $\frac{2}{5} = \frac{4}{......}$

(E_3) $\frac{6}{......} = \frac{12}{10}$

(E_4) $\frac{......}{2} = \frac{30}{12}$

(E_5) $\frac{......}{5} = \frac{20}{25}$

(E_6) $\frac{3}{7} = \frac{......}{56}$

(E_7) $\frac{9}{9} = \frac{54}{......}$

(E_8) $\frac{......}{2} = \frac{5}{10}$

(E_9) $\frac{3}{4} = \frac{......}{8}$

(E_{10}) $\frac{3}{8} = \frac{6}{......}$

(E_{11}) $\frac{......}{1} = \frac{27}{9}$

(E_{12}) $\frac{7}{4} = \frac{......}{40}$

(E_{13}) $\frac{6}{8} = \frac{36}{......}$

(E_{14}) $\frac{3}{......} = \frac{6}{14}$

(E_{15}) $\frac{......}{7} = \frac{27}{21}$

Answer Key	My Score
$(E_1) = 8$ $(E_2)=10$ $(E_3) = 5$ $(E_4)=5$ $(E_5)=4$ $(E_6) = 24$ $(E_7)=54$ $(E_8)=1$ $(E_9)=6$ $(E_{10})=16$ $(E_{11})=3$ $(E_{12})=70$ $(E_{13})=48$ $(E_{14})=7$ $(E_{15})=9$	/15

Equivalent

Name: ....

School: ....

DAY: 93

1) Find the equivalent fractions

Example: $\frac{1}{6} = \frac{....?}{60} = \frac{10}{60}$ (×10 numerator, ×10 denominator)

(E_1) $\frac{5}{9} = \frac{......}{9}$	(E_2) $\frac{6}{1} = \frac{42}{......}$	(E_3) $\frac{5}{......} = \frac{10}{10}$
(E_4) $\frac{......}{8} = \frac{10}{40}$	(E_5) $\frac{......}{3} = \frac{21}{21}$	(E_6) $\frac{2}{9} = \frac{......}{36}$
(E_7) $\frac{1}{7} = \frac{7}{......}$	(E_8) $\frac{......}{9} = \frac{18}{81}$	(E_9) $\frac{8}{1} = \frac{......}{3}$
(E_{10}) $\frac{5}{9} = \frac{5}{......}$	(E_{11}) $\frac{......}{9} = \frac{40}{72}$	(E_{12}) $\frac{9}{7} = \frac{......}{70}$
(E_{13}) $\frac{4}{5} = \frac{32}{......}$	(E_{14}) $\frac{1}{......} = \frac{4}{36}$	(E_{15}) $\frac{......}{2} = \frac{12}{12}$

Answer Key	My Score
$(E_1) = 5$ $(E_2)=7$ $(E_3) = 5$ $(E_4)=2$ $(E_5)=3$ $(E_6) = 8$ $(E_7)=49$ $(E_8)=2$ $(E_9)=24$ $(E_{10})=9$ $(E_{11})=5$ $(E_{12})=90$ $(E_{13})=40$ $(E_{14})=9$ $(E_{15})=2$	/15

Equivalent

Name: ....

School: ....

DAY: 94

1) Find the equivalent fractions

Example: $\frac{2}{8} = \frac{\dots?}{24} = \frac{6}{24}$ (×3 on the numerator, ×3 on the denominator)

(E_1) $\frac{5}{7} = \frac{\dots\dots}{28}$

(E_2) $\frac{6}{1} = \frac{24}{\dots\dots}$

(E_3) $\frac{8}{\dots\dots} = \frac{8}{4}$

(E_4) $\frac{\dots\dots}{4} = \frac{3}{4}$

(E_5) $\frac{\dots\dots}{7} = \frac{24}{28}$

(E_6) $\frac{8}{1} = \frac{\dots\dots}{5}$

(E_7) $\frac{9}{1} = \frac{27}{\dots\dots}$

(E_8) $\frac{\dots\dots}{3} = \frac{63}{27}$

(E_9) $\frac{2}{7} = \frac{\dots\dots}{63}$

(E_{10}) $\frac{7}{5} = \frac{56}{\dots\dots}$

(E_{11}) $\frac{\dots\dots}{8} = \frac{10}{16}$

(E_{12}) $\frac{9}{9} = \frac{\dots\dots}{81}$

(E_{13}) $\frac{8}{9} = \frac{32}{\dots\dots}$

(E_{14}) $\frac{1}{\dots\dots} = \frac{8}{56}$

(E_{15}) $\frac{\dots\dots}{1} = \frac{12}{6}$

Answer Key	My Score
$(E_1) = 20$ $(E_2)=4$ $(E_3) = 4$ $(E_4)=3$ $(E_5)=6$ $(E_6) = 40$ $(E_7)=3$ $(E_8)=7$ $(E_9)=18$ $(E_{10})=40$ $(E_{11})=5$ $(E_{12})=81$ $(E_{13})=36$ $(E_{14})=7$ $(E_{15})=2$	/15

Equivalent

Name: ....

School: ....

DAY: 95

1) Find the equivalent fractions

Example: $\frac{6}{9} = \frac{\ldots?}{72} = \frac{48}{72}$ (×8 on the numerator, ×8 on the denominator)

(E_1) $\frac{8}{5} = \frac{\ldots\ldots}{50}$

(E_2) $\frac{6}{6} = \frac{54}{\ldots\ldots}$

(E_3) $\frac{1}{\ldots\ldots} = \frac{1}{8}$

(E_4) $\frac{\ldots\ldots}{7} = \frac{72}{63}$

(E_5) $\frac{\ldots\ldots}{8} = \frac{27}{72}$

(E_6) $\frac{4}{5} = \frac{\ldots\ldots}{40}$

(E_7) $\frac{8}{7} = \frac{72}{\ldots\ldots}$

(E_8) $\frac{\ldots\ldots}{8} = \frac{56}{64}$

(E_9) $\frac{9}{5} = \frac{\ldots\ldots}{50}$

(E_{10}) $\frac{9}{4} = \frac{9}{\ldots\ldots}$

(E_{11}) $\frac{\ldots\ldots}{4} = \frac{2}{4}$

(E_{12}) $\frac{1}{6} = \frac{\ldots\ldots}{54}$

(E_{13}) $\frac{8}{7} = \frac{40}{\ldots\ldots}$

(E_{14}) $\frac{4}{\ldots\ldots} = \frac{36}{27}$

(E_{15}) $\frac{\ldots\ldots}{5} = \frac{4}{5}$

Answer Key	My Score
(E_{11})=2 (E_{12})=9 (E_{13})=35 (E_{14})=3 (E_{15})=4 (E_6) = 32 (E_7)=63 (E_8)=7 (E_9)=90 (E_{10})=4 (E_1) = 80 (E_2)=54 (E_3) = 8 (E_4)=8 (E_5)=3	/15

Equivalent

Name: ....

School: ....

DAY: 96

1) Find the equivalent fractions

Example: $\frac{8}{4} = \frac{....?}{8} = \frac{16}{8}$ (×2 numerator, ×2 denominator)

(E_1) $\frac{8}{7} = \frac{......}{70}$

(E_2) $\frac{2}{7} = \frac{6}{......}$

(E_3) $\frac{9}{......} = \frac{36}{32}$

(E_4) $\frac{......}{9} = \frac{12}{54}$

(E_5) $\frac{......}{9} = \frac{64}{72}$

(E_6) $\frac{4}{4} = \frac{......}{16}$

(E_7) $\frac{5}{4} = \frac{30}{......}$

(E_8) $\frac{......}{1} = \frac{4}{4}$

(E_9) $\frac{2}{4} = \frac{......}{32}$

(E_{10}) $\frac{6}{1} = \frac{30}{......}$

(E_{11}) $\frac{......}{2} = \frac{8}{2}$

(E_{12}) $\frac{8}{1} = \frac{......}{10}$

(E_{13}) $\frac{2}{9} = \frac{2}{......}$

(E_{14}) $\frac{5}{......} = \frac{5}{1}$

(E_{15}) $\frac{......}{8} = \frac{24}{48}$

Answer Key	My Score
(E_1) = 80 (E_2)=21 (E_3)= 8 (E_4)=2 (E_5)=8 (E_6) = 16 (E_7)=24 (E_8)=1 (E_9)=16 (E_{10})=5 (E_{11})=8 (E_{12})=80 (E_{13})=9 (E_{14})=1 (E_{15})=4	/15

Equivalent

Name: ....

School: ....

DAY: 97

1) Find the equivalent fractions

Example: $\frac{9}{7} = \frac{\dots?}{49} = \frac{63}{49}$ (×7 on numerator and denominator)

$(E_1)\ \frac{4}{9} = \frac{\dots\dots}{9}$

$(E_2)\ \frac{5}{8} = \frac{45}{\dots\dots}$

$(E_3)\ \frac{5}{\dots\dots} = \frac{50}{20}$

$(E_4)\ \frac{\dots\dots}{3} = \frac{6}{18}$

$(E_5)\ \frac{\dots\dots}{3} = \frac{2}{6}$

$(E_6)\ \frac{1}{6} = \frac{\dots\dots}{6}$

$(E_7)\ \frac{3}{6} = \frac{27}{\dots\dots}$

$(E_8)\ \frac{\dots\dots}{6} = \frac{32}{48}$

$(E_9)\ \frac{8}{6} = \frac{\dots\dots}{60}$

$(E_{10})\ \frac{6}{8} = \frac{6}{\dots\dots}$

$(E_{11})\ \frac{\dots\dots}{8} = \frac{4}{8}$

$(E_{12})\ \frac{9}{2} = \frac{\dots\dots}{10}$

$(E_{13})\ \frac{5}{9} = \frac{40}{\dots\dots}$

$(E_{14})\ \frac{1}{\dots\dots} = \frac{5}{45}$

$(E_{15})\ \frac{\dots\dots}{1} = \frac{8}{1}$

Answer Key	My Score
$(E_1) = 4$ $(E_2)=72$ $(E_3) = 2$ $(E_4)=1$ $(E_5)=1$ $(E_6) = 1$ $(E_7)=54$ $(E_8)=4$ $(E_9)=80$ $(E_{10})=8$ $(E_{11})=4$ $(E_{12})=45$ $(E_{13})=72$ $(E_{14})=9$ $(E_{15})=8$	/15

Equivalent

Name: ....

School: ....

DAY: 98

1) Find the equivalent fractions

Example: $\frac{6}{8} = \frac{....?}{48} = \frac{36}{48}$ (×6, ×6)

(E_1) $\frac{9}{5} = \frac{......}{35}$

(E_2) $\frac{2}{5} = \frac{10}{......}$

(E_3) $\frac{9}{......} = \frac{90}{20}$

(E_4) $\frac{......}{4} = \frac{7}{4}$

(E_5) $\frac{......}{9} = \frac{20}{90}$

(E_6) $\frac{4}{5} = \frac{......}{45}$

(E_7) $\frac{6}{9} = \frac{6}{......}$

(E_8) $\frac{......}{1} = \frac{5}{5}$

(E_9) $\frac{9}{6} = \frac{......}{30}$

(E_{10}) $\frac{6}{4} = \frac{42}{......}$

(E_{11}) $\frac{......}{8} = \frac{30}{80}$

(E_{12}) $\frac{9}{4} = \frac{......}{12}$

(E_{13}) $\frac{2}{5} = \frac{20}{......}$

(E_{14}) $\frac{7}{......} = \frac{7}{1}$

(E_{15}) $\frac{......}{2} = \frac{12}{6}$

Answer Key	My Score
(E_1) = 63 (E_2)=25 (E_3)= 2 (E_4)=7 (E_5)=2 (E_6) = 36 (E_7)=9 (E_8)=1 (E_9)=45 (E_{10})=28 (E_{11})=3 (E_{12})=27 (E_{13})=50 (E_{14})=1 (E_{15})=4	/15

Equivalent

Name: ....

School: ....

DAY: 99

1) Find the equivalent fractions

Example: $\frac{7}{9} = \frac{....?}{81} = \frac{63}{81}$ (numerator ×9, denominator ×9)

(E_1) $\frac{8}{1} = \frac{......}{4}$

(E_2) $\frac{9}{6} = \frac{18}{......}$

(E_3) $\frac{5}{......} = \frac{35}{7}$

(E_4) $\frac{......}{4} = \frac{9}{36}$

(E_5) $\frac{......}{2} = \frac{9}{6}$

(E_6) $\frac{2}{3} = \frac{......}{27}$

(E_7) $\frac{8}{3} = \frac{24}{......}$

(E_8) $\frac{......}{5} = \frac{8}{10}$

(E_9) $\frac{6}{3} = \frac{......}{24}$

(E_{10}) $\frac{2}{2} = \frac{18}{......}$

(E_{11}) $\frac{......}{2} = \frac{18}{18}$

(E_{12}) $\frac{9}{3} = \frac{......}{15}$

(E_{13}) $\frac{1}{6} = \frac{3}{......}$

(E_{14}) $\frac{3}{......} = \frac{6}{16}$

(E_{15}) $\frac{......}{5} = \frac{8}{40}$

Answer Key	My Score
$(E_1) = 32$ $(E_2)=12$ $(E_3) = 1$ $(E_4)=1$ $(E_5)=3$ $(E_6) = 18$ $(E_7)=9$ $(E_8)=4$ $(E_9)=48$ $(E_{10})=18$ $(E_{11})=2$ $(E_{12})=45$ $(E_{13})=18$ $(E_{14})=8$ $(E_{15})=1$	/15

Equivalent

Name: ....

School: ....

DAY: 100

1) Find the equivalent fractions

Example: $\frac{5}{1} = \frac{....?}{6} = \frac{30}{6}$ (×6, ×6)

$(E_1)\ \frac{9}{8} = \frac{......}{48}$ $(E_2)\ \frac{3}{5} = \frac{9}{......}$ $(E_3)\ \frac{7}{......} = \frac{42}{24}$

$(E_4)\ \frac{......}{8} = \frac{30}{40}$ $(E_5)\ \frac{......}{1} = \frac{48}{6}$ $(E_6)\ \frac{4}{4} = \frac{......}{36}$

$(E_7)\ \frac{2}{6} = \frac{6}{......}$ $(E_8)\ \frac{......}{3} = \frac{10}{30}$ $(E_9)\ \frac{6}{6} = \frac{......}{30}$

$(E_{10})\ \frac{8}{1} = \frac{16}{......}$ $(E_{11})\ \frac{......}{3} = \frac{30}{18}$ $(E_{12})\ \frac{4}{1} = \frac{......}{7}$

$(E_{13})\ \frac{5}{8} = \frac{15}{......}$ $(E_{14})\ \frac{4}{......} = \frac{16}{32}$ $(E_{15})\ \frac{......}{8} = \frac{18}{24}$

Answer Key	My Score
$(E_1) = 54$ $(E_2)=15$ $(E_3) = 4$ $(E_4)=6$ $(E_5)=8$ $(E_6) = 36$ $(E_7)=18$ $(E_8)=1$ $(E_9)=30$ $(E_{10})=2$ $(E_{11})=5$ $(E_{12})=28$ $(E_{13})=24$ $(E_{14})=8$ $(E_{15})=6$	/15

Printed in Great Britain
by Amazon

21767773R00057

Answers

Section One — The Design Process

Page 4 — Product and Market Analysis — 1

1 E.g. any two of: the cost of the product *[1 mark]* / nutritional information *[1 mark]* / storage/cooking instructions *[1 mark]* / suitability for different consumers, e.g. vegetarians *[1 mark]*.

2 a) The group of people the company want to sell the product to *[1 mark]*.

b) i) E.g. the product should contain no meat *[1 mark]*.

ii) E.g. the product should be quick to prepare/easy to eat/available in ready-made portions *[1 mark]*.

3 a) Snack B *[1 mark]*.

b) E.g. adults/health-conscious people/people on a calorie-controlled diet *[1 mark]* because the product has a sensible name *[1 mark]* / uses sensible text on the packaging *[1 mark]* / states its nutritional content *[1 mark]* / uses sensible graphics on the packaging *[1 mark]*. *[1 mark for a sensible target group, up to 2 marks for a detailed reason]*

Page 5 — Product and Market Analysis — 2

4 a) E.g. to find ways of improving their product *[1 mark]*.

b) E.g. the packaging of both products show fun graphics which will appeal to children. / Product A contains a free cartoon which will also appeal to children *[1 mark]*. Both cereals are sweet which will appeal to many children — product A contains chocolate drops and product B contains honey covered oats *[1 mark]*. Both cereals are relatively healthy, which will appeal to parents — product A has high levels of potassium and calcium which are important for growth, especially in children. Product B contains lots of fruit (and therefore many vitamins and minerals) and has no added sugar *[1 mark]*.

c) E.g. Product B
Improvement: Include some marshmallows *[1 mark]*
Explanation: It will make the cereal more appealing to children *[1 mark]*.

Page 6 — Market Research — 1

1 The texture *[1 mark]* and colour *[1 mark]* of the pastry.

2 a) Because they are the people who the new product is aimed at *[1 mark]*, so their opinions will influence the development of the product *[1 mark]*.

b) E.g. the results can be easier to analyse *[1 mark]*.

c) E.g. any two of: fewer human errors are made *[1 mark]* / the results can easily be copied/shared/changed/presented/compared *[1 mark]* / results look neater *[1 mark]* / a range of graphics/presenting methods can be used *[1 mark]*.

Page 7 — Market Research — 2

3 Because testers could tell the difference between the low-fat yogurt and the full-fat yogurt samples *[1 mark]*. The company might re-design the low-fat yogurt so that it's more similar to the full-fat yogurt/so that testers are unable to tell the difference *[1 mark]*.

4 a) E.g. they could research what qualities make Product B the most preferred cheesecake *[1 mark]* and try to improve their product to be more like Product B *[1 mark]*.

b) A rating test involves asking people to give each product a rating, e.g. from 1 to 10 *[1 mark]*.
A ranking test involves asking people to rank products in their order of preference *[1 mark]*.

Page 8 — Market Research — 3

5 a) Rating how good samples of food are using different senses, e.g. taste, smell *[1 mark]*.

b) E.g. it helps manufacturers to find out what consumers think about various aspects of their product *[1 mark]*.
It helps manufacturers to identify which aspects of their product they should improve so that consumers will be more likely to buy the product *[1 mark]*.
It helps manufacturers to compare their product with other products/brands *[1 mark]*.

c) E.g. any three of: they can use a large group of testers *[1 mark]*. / Codes/symbols for the products so testers aren't influenced by the name or packaging *[1 mark]*. / Clean spoons for each test *[1 mark]*. / Water for testers to drink between tests *[1 mark]*.

6 E.g. any four of: the results show consumers thought that puff pastry has a better texture, but flaky pastry has a better flavour, moistness and overall appearance *[1 mark]*. / Both pastries scored the same for their colour *[1 mark]*. / The flaky pastry scored higher in most of the categories so is probably more suitable to use for sausage rolls *[1 mark]*. / The manufacturer could use the results to further improve the flaky pastry, e.g. improve its texture *[1 mark]*. / The manufacturer could compare the results with previous/future sensory tests with target consumers *[1 mark]*.

Page 9 — Design Criteria

1 E.g. any three of: what type/brand of rice consumers prefer *[1 mark]*. / How much consumers spend on rice-based products *[1 mark]*. / How popular rice-based dishes are *[1 mark]*. / How popular ready-made meals are *[1 mark]*. / How long people want to spend cooking a meal *[1 mark]*. / If target consumers are concerned with healthy eating *[1 mark]*.

2 E.g. any four of: the product should be a potato crisp product *[1 mark]*. / Have an exotic/multiculturally-influenced flavour *[1 mark]*. / Have a similar texture to potato crisps *[1 mark]*. / Be low in calories *[1 mark]*. / Be high in nutrients *[1 mark]*. / Cost around 50p *[1 mark]*.

3 E.g. any three of: Appealing to children *[1 mark]*. / Easy to eat *[1 mark]*. / Low in sugar *[1 mark]*. / High in vitamins/minerals/fibre/protein *[1 mark]*. / Contains carbohydrate for slow-release energy *[1 mark]*. / Small portion size *[1 mark]*. / Fairly cheap *[1 mark]*. / No artificial additives *[1 mark]*.

Page 10 — Generating Proposals — 1

1 Idea 1 *[1 mark]* because it meets more of the design criteria *[1 mark]*.

2 a) The product contain nuts so meets one of the design criteria *[1 mark]*. But it doesn't meet any other design criteria because it uses a caramel filling and luxury Belgian chocolate which aren't cheap *[1 mark]*, it has sugar-coated nuts and a caramel filling so it isn't low in sugar *[1 mark]* and it uses milk chocolate so it isn't free from dairy products *[1 mark]*.

Answers

b) E.g. they could use cheaper chocolate and remove the caramel filling to reduce the cost of the product ***[1 mark]***. They could use a sugar substitute in their chocolate/not coat the nuts in sugar/remove the caramel filling to reduce the sugar content ***[1 mark]***. They could use dairy-free chocolate instead of milk chocolate ***[1 mark]***.

Page 11 — Generating Proposals — 2

3 a) Notes / sketch should show:
- a soup-based product ***[1 mark]***.
- soup with a smooth texture, e.g. mention blending ingredients ***[1 mark]***.
- the soup is suitable for batch production, e.g. common ingredients that can be bought in bulk and simple production method ***[1 mark]***.
- soup containing at least one portion of fruit or vegetables ***[1 mark]***.
- the soup is suitable for consumers with a special diet, e.g. vegetarians ***[1 mark]***.
- a product that provides sensory appeal, e.g. flavour, texture, aroma ***[1 mark]***.

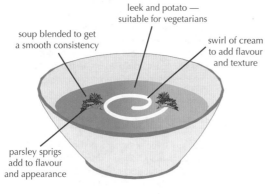

E.g. leek and potato soup:

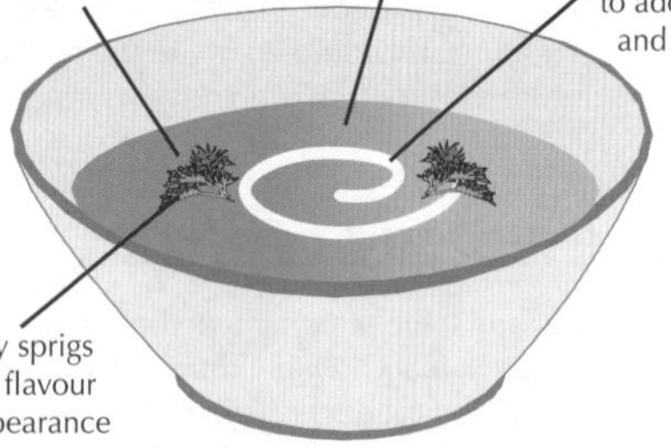

b) E.g. the software could be used to check the nutritional content of the ingredients ***[1 mark]***, to check any nutritional losses that will occur due to cooking ***[1 mark]*** and to check the final product meets the design criteria/recommended guidelines for the target market ***[1 mark]***.

Page 12 — Generating Proposals — 3

4 Notes / annotated sketches should both show:
- a pastry-based product ***[1 mark]***.
- a savoury filling ***[1 mark]***.
- suitability for vegetarians, e.g. no meat used ***[1 mark]***.
- have a suitable glazed finish, e.g. brushed with egg ***[1 mark]***.
- a product that provides sensory appeal, e.g. flavour, texture, aroma ***[1 mark]***.

[Maximum of 5 marks available for each design.]

E.g. mushroom and leek pie:

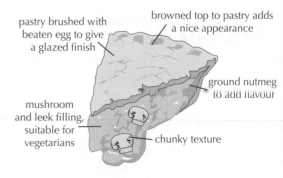

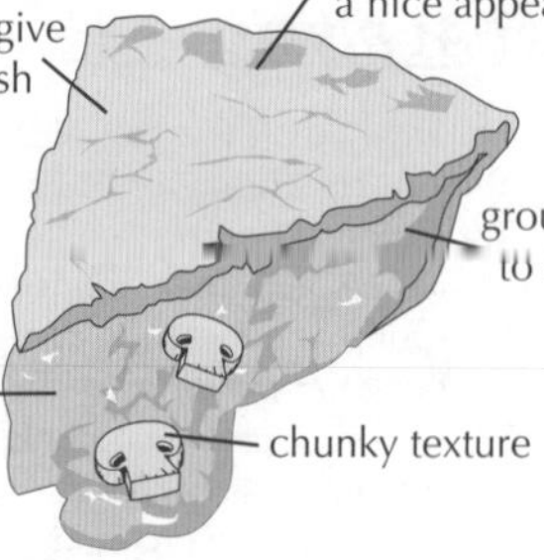

E.g. mushroom and asparagus quiche:

Page 13 — Product Specification — 1

1 a) A detailed list/description of what the product is like ***[1 mark]***.

b) E.g. any two of: because you need to check the product meets the design criteria and the design brief ***[1 mark]***. / To identify any potential improvements ***[1 mark]***. / To check the product will sell well to your target market ***[1 mark]***.

c) E.g. they could make the product and conduct a taste test ***[1 mark]***.

2 E.g. no-one can steal their idea if it has been registered ***[1 mark]***. They can make money from their idea ***[1 mark]***.

3 E.g.
1. Each biscuit will/must weigh 100 g ± 5 g ***[1 mark]***.
2. Each biscuit will have 10 g ± 1 g sugar ***[1 mark]***.
3. The manufacturing cost of each biscuit will be 10p ***[1 mark]***.

Page 14 — Product Specification — 2

4 a) Notes / annotated sketches should show:
- a savoury meal for one person ***[1 mark]***.
- a tomato-based sauce, e.g. tomato and herb ***[1 mark]***.
- a high carbohydrate meal that uses pasta ***[1 mark]***.
- a meal high in protein, e.g. uses meat or an alternative protein, e.g. beans, lentils ***[1 mark]***.
- a product that provides sensory appeal, e.g. flavour, texture, aroma ***[1 mark]***.

Answers

E.g. spaghetti bolognese:

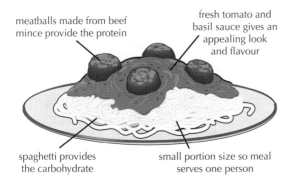

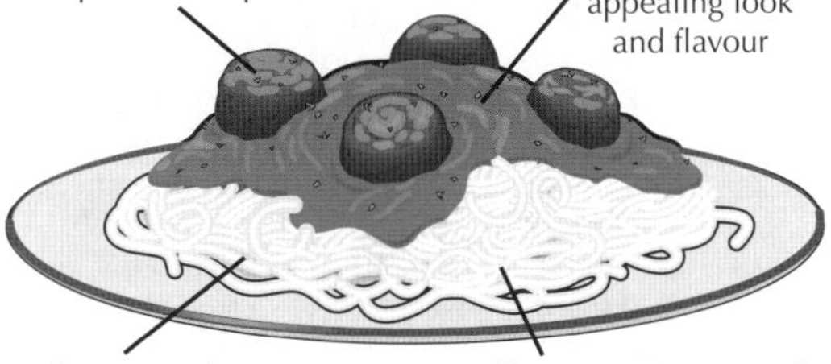

b) E.g. each portion size will be 250 g ± 5 g ***[1 mark]***. Each portion will contain 100 g ± 3 g spaghetti ***[1 mark]***. Each portion will have 5 mince beef meatballs weighing 20 g ± 2 g each ***[1 mark]***. Each portion will have 50 ml ± 5 ml tomato and basil sauce ***[1 mark]***. The manufacturing cost of each portion will be 75p ***[1 mark]***.

Page 15 — Development — 1

1 a) E.g. use cheaper/lower quality ingredients / use less chicken in the sandwich / decrease portion size ***[1 mark]***.

b) E.g. the product might have a less appealing flavour/look/texture / might have to be sold at a lower price ***[1 mark]***.

2 E.g. any two of: use more fat in the cake ***[1 mark]***. / Reduce the cooking time ***[1 mark]***. / Bake the cake in a deeper tray ***[1 mark]***. / Use a syrup finish which will soak into the sponge cake and moisten it ***[1 mark]***.

3 a) Use gluten-free flour ***[1 mark]***.

b) E.g. increase the proportion of apples/add other fruits high in vitamin C to the product / reduce the cooking time of the apples/change the cooking method so that less vitamin C is lost ***[1 mark]***.

Page 16 — Development — 2

4 a) E.g. use lower fat ingredients, e.g. lean mince ***[1 mark]***, use a healthier cooking method ***[1 mark]***.

b) Reduce the cooking time ***[1 mark]***, reduce the cooking temperature ***[1 mark]***.

c) It allows the manufacturer to discover and solve any potential problems, so that they can improve the product ***[1 mark]*** and make sure that the final design is the best design possible and the most likely to be successful ***[1 mark]***.

5 a) The taste might be affected by using less golden syrup ***[1 mark]***. Using less golden syrup/butter may result in a drier texture/the flapjack not being as chewy ***[1 mark]***. But using less golden syrup and butter will make the product lower in sugar and fat ***[1 mark]***.

b) E.g. use low-sugar golden syrup / low-fat spread / reduce the portion size ***[1 mark]***.

Page 17 — Development — 3

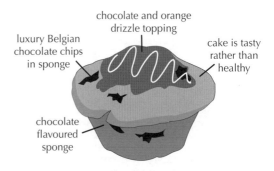

6 a) Annotated sketch should show:
- chocolate flavour ***[1 mark]***.
- chocolate and / or orange topping ***[1 mark]***.
- the flavour of the cake being more important than its healthiness ***[1 mark]***.

E.g. chocolate chip muffin:

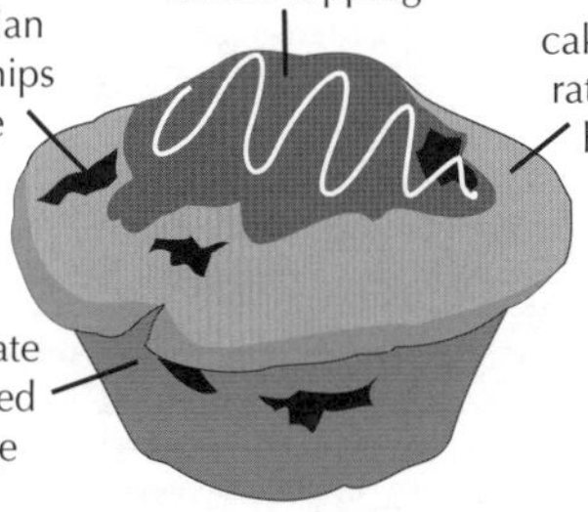

b) E.g. the design idea takes into account consumer preferences from market research ***[1 mark]***. / The product could be adapted for consumers who are lactose-intolerant by not having any dairy products in the ingredients, e.g. use dairy-free chocolate ***[1 mark]***. / No artificial additives would be used in case consumers are allergic to them ***[1 mark]***. / The product could be adapted for consumers who are coeliacs by using gluten-free flour ***[1 mark]***. / The muffins would be made in an area where there were no products containing nuts so they would be suitable for consumers with nut allergies ***[1 mark]***.
[1 mark for analysis against interview results. 1 mark for each relevant point about adapting the product, up to 3 marks.]

Page 18 — Manufacturer's Specification — 1

1 E.g. in a Gantt chart ***[1 mark]***.

2 E.g. to test the instructions are clear and detailed enough for every stage ***[1 mark]***. To test that the final product meets the design criteria ***[1 mark]***.

3 a) 22 g ***[1 mark]***.

b) It doesn't provide enough information ***[1 mark]*** because it doesn't include costings / quality control / detailed making instructions / etc. ***[1 mark]***.

c) It will make it cheaper ***[1 mark]*** because of discounts for buying ingredients in bulk / production lines can be cheaper ***[1 mark]***.

Page 19 — Manufacturer's Specification — 2

4 E.g. any three of: a precise description of how to make the product ***[1 mark]***. / A list of ingredients with precise amounts ***[1 mark]***. / The dimensions of the product in mm ***[1 mark]***. / Product tolerances ***[1 mark]*** / finishing details ***[1 mark]***. / Quality control instructions ***[1 mark]***. / Costings ***[1 mark]***.

Answers

5 Flowchart should show:

- A clear, logical order ***[1 mark]***.
- Quality control checks, e.g. size, shape ***[1 mark]***.
- Safety control checks, e.g. personal/kitchen/food hygiene ***[1 mark]***.
- Feedback from control checks ***[1 mark]***.
- Key times ***[1 mark]***.
- Key temperatures ***[1 mark]***.

E.g. flowchart:

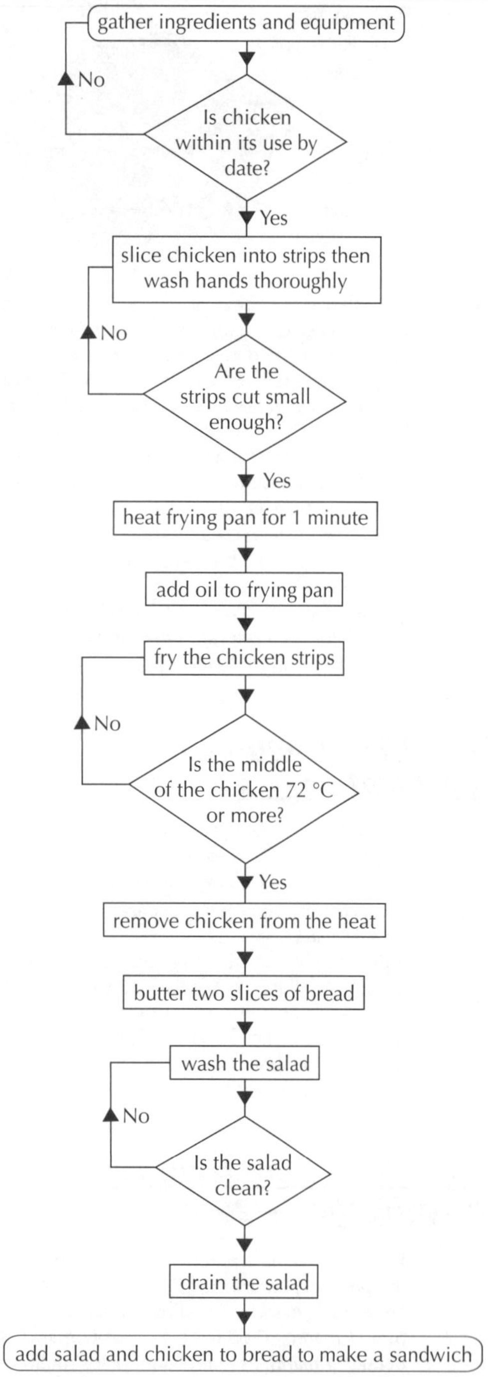

Section Two — Properties of Food

Page 20 — Carbohydrates — Sugar

1 a) Caramelisation ***[1 mark]***.

b) Jam — to preserve / to sweeten ***[1 mark]***.
Bread — to speed up fermentation ***[1 mark]***.

2 a) Caster sugar ***[1 mark]*** — e.g. because it will give the sponge a smooth texture / it has finer granules ***[1 mark]***.

b) Icing sugar ***[1 mark]*** — e.g. because it instantly dissolves in water to form a smooth paste / it's a fine powder so it can be dusted over cakes easily ***[1 mark]***.

3 a) It provides energy ***[1 mark]***.

b) E.g. any two of: to appeal to consumers on a calorie controlled diet ***[1 mark]***. / To appeal to consumers who want a better drink for their teeth ***[1 mark]***. / To appeal to people with diabetes ***[1 mark]***.

Page 21 — Carbohydrates — Starch — 1

1 a) E.g. any two of: flour ***[1 mark]*** / rice ***[1 mark]*** / bread ***[1 mark]*** / pasta ***[1 mark]***.

b) It provides energy ***[1 mark]***.

2 Pasta — starch acts as a bulking agent ***[1 mark]***. The starch granules swell when a liquid is added ***[1 mark]***.
White sauce — starch acts as a thickening agent ***[1 mark]***. When heat is applied to a starch and liquid mixture, gelatinisation occurs and thickens the sauce ***[1 mark]***.

3 a) i) Starch that has been treated so that it reacts in a particular way in certain conditions ***[1 mark]***.

ii) E.g. the starch has already gelatinised so the noodles and sauce thicken instantly ***[1 mark]***.

b) E.g. food will keep its moisture ***[1 mark]*** and nutrients ***[1 mark]*** when reheated.

Page 22 — Carbohydrates — Starch — 2

4 a) i) Strong flour ***[1 mark]***.

ii) Gluten ***[1 mark]***.

iii) To make the dough rise / to produce carbon dioxide ***[1 mark]***.

b) E.g. nuts / raisins / cinnamon / etc. ***[1 mark]***.

c) Notes / sketch and annotations should show:

- a savoury bread product ***[1 mark]***.
- a product suitable for a eating without cutlery, e.g. small size, hand-held, not sticky ***[1 mark]***.
- a product that provides sensory appeal, e.g. flavour, texture, aroma ***[1 mark]***.

E.g. cinnamon and raisin bagel:

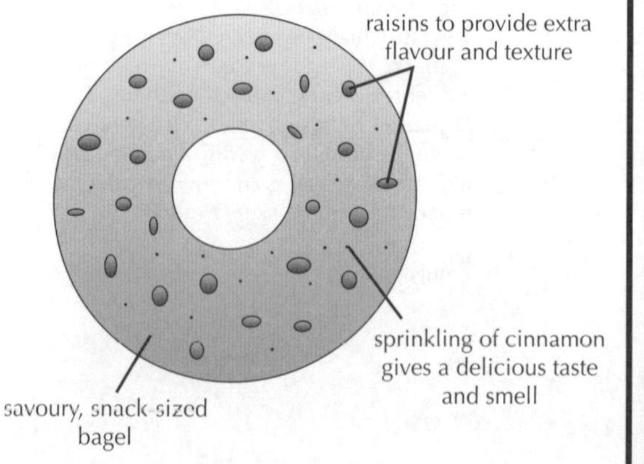

Answers

Page 23 — Proteins — Meat, Poultry and Fish

1 a) i) E.g. beef / lamb / pork ***[1 mark]***.
ii) E.g. chicken / turkey ***[1 mark]***.
iii) E.g. salmon / cod / lobster ***[1 mark]***.
iv) E.g. tofu / TVP / Quorn™ ***[1 mark]***.
b) Protein helps the body to grow ***[1 mark]*** and to repair muscles and tissues ***[1 mark]***. Proteins are made of amino acids, and some proteins contain essential amino acids which the body can't make itself ***[1 mark]***.
2 Marinate the meat in something acidic, to soften the texture by breaking down the fibres ***[1 mark]***. Hit the meat with a steak mallet to partly break down the fibres and make the meat more tender ***[1 mark]***.
3 Notes / sketch and annotations should show:
- a savoury meal ***[1 mark]***.
- a product suitable for a vegetarian ***[1 mark]***.
- a high-protein meal, e.g. containing Quorn™, TVP, tofu ***[1 mark]***.
- a product that provides sensory appeal, e.g. flavour, texture, aroma ***[1 mark]***.

E.g. vegetarian lasagne:

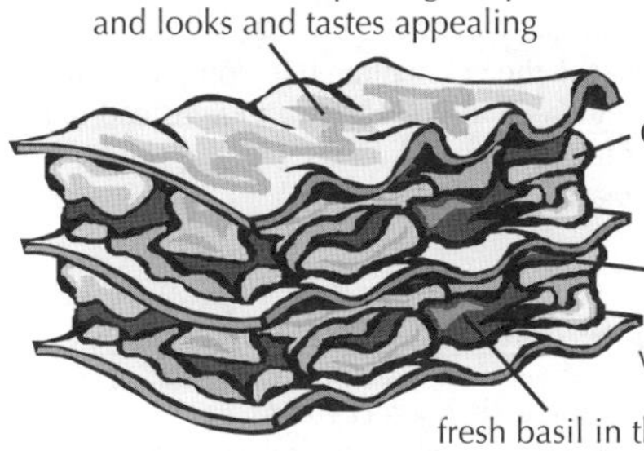

Page 24 — Proteins — Eggs — 1

1 a) Brushing a beaten egg mixture over a product ***[1 mark]***.
b) E.g. to give their products a glossy finish / to make their products look more attractive ***[1 mark]***.
2 E.g. fat ***[1 mark]***, vitamin A/B2/D ***[1 mark]***, iodine ***[1 mark]***.
3 a) Because they absorb a lot of the fat/oil they're cooked in ***[1 mark]***.
b) Any two of: by using oils that contain unsaturated fats ***[1 mark]*** / by draining off as much of the oil as possible before eating the eggs ***[1 mark]*** / by using less oil for cooking the eggs ***[1 mark]***.
c) Any two of: poaching ***[1 mark]*** / boiling ***[1 mark]*** / scrambling ***[1 mark]***.

Page 25 — Proteins — Eggs — 2

4 Coagulation — eggs become more solid at high temperatures ***[1 mark]***, then set and stay thickened ***[1 mark]***.
Emulsification — egg yolks contain lecithin ***[1 mark]***, which keeps emulsions stable / stops emulsions from separating ***[1 mark]***.
Aeration — e.g. when egg white is beaten, the protein in it is stretched ***[1 mark]*** and air becomes trapped ***[1 mark]***.

5 a) E.g. salmonella ***[1 mark]***.
b) E.g. manufacturers should make sure that eggs are thoroughly cooked so that all bacteria are destroyed ***[1 mark]***. Dried or pasteurised eggs can be used in products like mayonnaise, to make sure they're safe ***[1 mark]***.

Page 26 — Fats and Oils — 1

1 a) Any one of: meat / butter / suet / dripping / lard ***[1 mark]***.
b) Any one of: peanut oil / sunflower oil / corn oil / soya oil / rapeseed oil / olive oil ***[1 mark]***.
c) Unsaturated fat ***[1 mark]*** as it is associated with lower cholesterol levels ***[1 mark]***.
2 It is a source of energy ***[1 mark]***, a source of vitamin A/D/E/K ***[1 mark]***, it provides fatty acids ***[1 mark]***.
3 a) E.g. they could add less fat to their pastry mixture ***[1 mark]***. This would mean more gluten could be produced when mixing the flour and other ingredients ***[1 mark]*** so the pastry would stick together better ***[1 mark]***.
b) Butter ***[1 mark]***.
c) E.g. to improve the flavour ***[1 mark]***.
d) E.g. any one of: to enrich the sauce / to thicken the sauce / to add flavour ***[1 mark]***.

Page 27 — Fats and Oils — 2

4 a) E.g. to add flavour ***[1 mark]***, to add colour ***[1 mark]***.
b) Because lard is made from pig fat ***[1 mark]*** and vegetarians don't eat any meat or animal products ***[1 mark]***.
c) E.g. any one of: sunflower oil / rapeseed oil / olive oil / corn oil / soya oil ***[1 mark]***.
5 a) Sales of lard have decreased ***[1 mark]***.
b) E.g. any three of: lard contains saturated fats, which are unhealthy ***[1 mark]***. / Saturated fats are associated with high levels of cholesterol, which can increase the risk of heart disease ***[1 mark]***. / People in the UK are becoming more health conscious so are likely to switch from using lard to using low-fat spreads or oils ***[1 mark]***. / There were more vegetarians in the UK in the 1990s than in the 1950s ***[1 mark]***.

Page 28 — Vitamins and Minerals — 1

1 a) E.g. dark green vegetables ***[1 mark]***.
b) E.g. it's needed to form haemoglobin/blood ***[1 mark]***.
c) E.g. anaemia ***[1 mark]***.
2 a) Vitamin B Group: Food sources — any two of: cereals ***[1 mark]*** / liver ***[1 mark]*** / kidney ***[1 mark]*** / peas ***[1 mark]*** / pulses ***[1 mark]*** / dairy produce ***[1 mark]*** / meat ***[1 mark]*** / fish ***[1 mark]***. Function — any one of: helps the nervous system / helps with the release of energy from carbohydrates / helps with the repair of tissues / helps with tissue growth ***[1 mark]***.
b) Vitamin C (ascorbic acid): Food sources — any two of: citrus fruits ***[1 mark]*** / green vegetables ***[1 mark]*** / peppers ***[1 mark]*** / potatoes ***[1 mark]***. Function — any one of: protects the body from infection/allergies / helps in the absorption of calcium and iron from food / helps to keep blood vessels healthy / helps to heal wounds ***[1 mark]***.

Answers

3 a) E.g. any three of: cook the carrots as quickly as possible in a small amount of water *[1 mark]*. / Don't leave the carrots to stand in water *[1 mark]*. / Steam or microwave the carrots to keep in more of the nutrients *[1 mark]*. / Cut carrots into bigger slices so they have a smaller surface area, so fewer nutrients are lost when they're cooked *[1 mark]*. / Peel the carrots very thinly *[1 mark]*. / Wash but don't peel the carrots, to keep the nutrients and fibre found in the skin *[1 mark]*.

b) No effect / no nutrients are lost *[1 mark]*.

Page 29 — Vitamins and Minerals — 2

4 a) E.g. calcium is needed for strong bones and teeth *[1 mark]*, and healthy nerves and muscles *[1 mark]*.

b) i) E.g. any one of: oily fish / eggs *[1 mark]*.

ii) E.g. any one of: milk / tofu / salmon / green leafy vegetables / white bread / cheese *[1 mark]*.

c) Rickets / osteoporosis *[1 mark]*.

5 Flowchart, notes and / or diagrams should show:

- a fruit salad consisting of bananas, apples, oranges and kiwi fruits *[1 mark]*.
- a clear, logical order, e.g. fruit stored, prepared and then used *[1 mark]*.
- personal hygiene and safety considerations *[1 mark]*.
- Clear explanations of how to store fruit to minimise loss of nutrients, e.g. store in a cool, dark place / store apples, oranges and kiwi fruits in a larder or a fridge / don't store bananas in the fridge *[1 mark]*.
- Clear explanations of how to prepare fruit to minimise loss of nutrients, e.g. wash but don't peel the apples to keep the nutrients and fibre found just below the skin *[1 mark]*.

Page 30 — Additives — 1

1 a) To enhance the flavour *[1 mark]*.

b) E.g. sauces / soups / crisps *[1 mark]*.

2 a) E.g. because customers don't tend to like the idea of artificial additives, so are more likely to buy products containing natural additives *[1 mark]*.

b) i) Any two of: salt *[1 mark]*, sugar *[1 mark]*, caramel *[1 mark]*.

ii) Saccharin *[1 mark]*, vanilla essence *[1 mark]*.

c) E.g. to add flavour *[1 mark]*, to add colour *[1 mark]*.

3 The additive has passed a safety test *[1 mark]* and can be used throughout the European Union *[1 mark]*.

Page 31 — Additives — 2

4 a) E.g. vinegar *[1 mark]* is used to pickle eggs *[1 mark]*. / Concentrated lemon juice *[1 mark]* is used to keep salads fresh *[1 mark]*. / Salt *[1 mark]* is used to cure meat *[1 mark]*. / Sugar *[1 mark]* is used to preserve jam *[1 mark]*.

b) E.g. lecithin *[1 mark]* is used to keep mayonnaise stable *[1 mark]*.

c) E.g. gelatine *[1 mark]* is used to thicken jelly so that it sets as a gel *[1 mark]*.

d) E.g. yeast *[1 mark]* is used to make bread rise *[1 mark]*. / Baking powder/bicarbonate of soda *[1 mark]* is used to make cakes rise *[1 mark]*.

5 Answer should include a range of advantages and disadvantages, e.g. additives have many uses and can improve the properties of food, from improving its taste/texture/colour *[1 mark]* to extending its shelf life *[1 mark]*. But no-one is certain of the long-term health effects of additives yet *[1 mark]*. Some people think eating artificial additives could be linked to behavioural problems, e.g. hyperactivity *[1 mark]*. If eaten in large amounts some additives, like sugar and salt, are bad for our health *[1 mark]*. They can also disguise poor quality ingredients *[1 mark]*, e.g. processed meat products may not contain much meat but they can be made to taste good, by using additives.

Page 32 — Acids and Alkalis — 1

1 a) Lactic acid *[1 mark]*.

b) Because the acid will give yogurt a sour taste *[1 mark]*.

2 a) i) It will give the meringue a softer, chewier texture *[1 mark]* because vinegar partly breaks down the proteins in the egg white, which changes the texture *[1 mark]*.

ii) Any two of: to tenderise/soften meat, e.g. in a marinade *[1 mark]*. / To give foods a sharp flavour, e.g. in salad dressings *[1 mark]*. / To preserve foods, e.g. in chutneys *[1 mark]*.

iii) Cornflour *[1 mark]*.

b) Because the concentrated lemon juice will help the fruit to keep its colour *[1 mark]*, instead of the fruit turning brown as it reacts with oxygen in the air *[1 mark]*.

Page 33 — Acids and Alkalis — 2

3 a) Bicarbonate of soda *[1 mark]*.

b) It breaks down when heated to produce carbon dioxide *[1 mark]*. The carbon dioxide bubbles expand and make mixtures rise *[1 mark]*.

c) Alkalis have an unpleasant, bitter taste *[1 mark]*.

d) Any two strongly flavoured products, e.g. gingerbread *[1 mark]*, chocolate cake *[1 mark]*. The taste of the alkali would not be a problem because the strong flavour of the product would mask the unpleasant taste *[1 mark]*.

4 Notes / sketch and annotations should show:

- a suitable dessert product *[1 mark]*.
- acid clearly identified *[1 mark]* and an explanation given *[1 mark]*.
- alkali clearly identified *[1 mark]* and an explanation given *[1 mark]*.

E.g. strawberry chocolate gateaux:

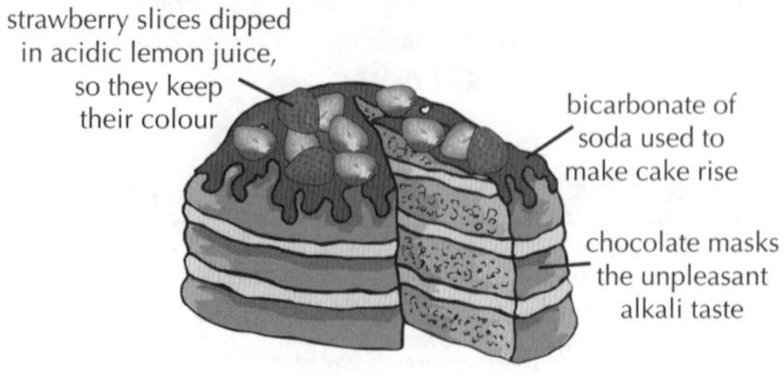

Answers

Page 34 — Healthy Eating — 1

1 The guideline recommends everyone eats at least five portions of fruit and vegetables every day ***[1 mark]***.

2 a) Any two of: include fruit and vegetables in the diet ***[1 mark]***. / Reduce the amount of fatty foods eaten ***[1 mark]***. / Reduce the amount of sugary foods eaten ***[1 mark]***. / Eat more starchy foods ***[1 mark]***.

b) Chocolate bar ***[1 mark]***.

3 a) Any one of: high blood pressure / heart disease / stroke ***[1 mark]***.

b) Any one of: obesity / heart disease / cancer ***[1 mark]***.

c) Any one of: obesity / Type 2 diabetes / tooth decay ***[1 mark]***.

Page 35 — Healthy Eating — 2

4 a) i) The mince could be replaced with tofu / Quorn™ / vegetables ***[1 mark]***. It could be served with no cheese on the top ***[1 mark]***.

ii) The spaghetti could be replaced with gluten-free spaghetti ***[1 mark]***.

iii) The product could be prepared using ingredients that do not contain nuts or traces of nuts ***[1 mark]***.

b) i) Lactose intolerance ***[1 mark]***.

ii) The grated cheese ***[1 mark]***.

5 Notes / sketch and annotations should show a suitably adapted sponge based product.
3 marks for 3 different ways of cutting calories, e.g:

- less cream used / low-fat cream used ***[1 mark]***.
- low-sugar jam used / jam replaced with fresh fruit ***[1 mark]***.
- portion size reduced ***[1 mark]***.
- reduced fat/sugar sponge cake ***[1 mark]***.
- sugar substitute used that is lower in calories ***[1 mark]***.

Page 36 — New Technology — 1

1 a) Genetically modified ***[1 mark]***.

b) A food that has had its genes altered ***[1 mark]*** to give it useful characteristics ***[1 mark]***.

2 a) Some consumers may believe that altering genes is not natural ***[1 mark]***. They might be concerned about any long-term health effects of GM foods, which aren't currently known ***[1 mark]***.

b) E.g. all GM foods must undergo strict safety assessments and they can only be sold if they're found to have no health risks / all foods that are GM or contain more than 1% GM ingredients must be clearly labelled ***[1 mark]***.

3 E.g. any one of: packaging with protection against moisture can slow down the growth of bacteria on foods, so they last for longer. / Breathable packaging can help keep fruit fresher for longer. / Vacuum packaging can extend the shelf life of dry foods ***[1 mark]***.

Page 37 — New Technology — 2

4 a) A food that has been artificially modified ***[1 mark]*** to provide a particular health benefit, on top of its normal nutritional value ***[1 mark]***.

b) E.g. any two of: fruit juices with added calcium ***[1 mark]***. / Eggs with added omega-3 ***[1 mark]***. / Golden Rice/bread with added vitamins ***[1 mark]***. / Margarine with added omega-3/vitamins ***[1 mark]***.

c) Functional foods mean people with a poor diet can easily eat more of a certain nutrient ***[1 mark]***.
People who can't eat particular foods can get the nutrients they lack by eating functional foods ***[1 mark]***.
Some functional foods could help solve some health problems caused by malnutrition in poor countries ***[1 mark]***.

5 Advantages — e.g. farmers can use GM crops that will grow quicker than normal crops ***[1 mark]***. If farmers plant GM maize that is pest-resistant, they will get a bigger yield of maize because less of the crop will be eaten or damaged by pests ***[1 mark]***. This makes it cheaper for the farmer to produce ***[1 mark]*** and so makes it cheaper for the consumer to buy ***[1 mark]***. The consumer benefits because foods can be made to ripen earlier in the year, when they wouldn't normally be available ***[1 mark]***, and their shelf life can be increased ***[1 mark]***.
[1 mark for each advantage, up to 3 marks].
Disadvantages — e.g. GM producers can't sell their food everywhere because of EU restrictions ***[1 mark]***. The long-term health effects of GM foods aren't yet known ***[1 mark]***, and there are concerns that modified genes could get out into the wider environment and cause environmental problems ***[1 mark]***.
[1 mark for each disadvantage, up to 3 marks].

Section Three — Food Processes

Page 38 — Combining Ingredients — 1

1 A solid held in a liquid ***[1 mark]***, which doesn't dissolve ***[1 mark]***.

2 a) A solution ***[1 mark]***.

b) Pectin helps to set the jam / make a thick solution / causes gelatinisation ***[1 mark]***.

3 a) Egg yolk / lecithin ***[1 mark]***.

b) An emulsion is formed when oily and watery liquids are mixed together ***[1 mark]*** and are held together / prevented from separating by an emulsifier ***[1 mark]***.

c) E.g. vinaigrette ***[1 mark]***.

Page 39 — Combining Ingredients — 2

4 a) E.g. caster sugar has fine grains and creams easily, giving the cake a light texture ***[1 mark]***. Using a dark brown sugar would change the colour/texture/flavour of the cake ***[1 mark]***.

b) E.g. any two of: beat the egg whites for longer ***[1 mark]***. / Fold the flour into the mixture instead of beating it ***[1 mark]***. / Add a raising agent ***[1 mark]***. / Use self-raising flour ***[1 mark]***.

c) i) It may change the flavour/texture/appearance ***[1 mark]***.

ii) E.g. using less sugar / replacing sugar with another sweet ingredient such as fruit / using sugar substitutes/ artificial sweeteners ***[1 mark]***.

5 a) E.g. adding more salt ***[1 mark]***. Adding some herbs or spices ***[1 mark]***.

b) i) E.g. low-salt diets ***[1 mark]***. / Low-fat diets ***[1 mark]***. / Gluten-free diets ***[1 mark]***. / Vegetarian diets ***[1 mark]***.

ii) E.g. reducing the amount of salt in the sauce ***[1 mark]*** and replacing it with herbs to add flavour ***[1 mark]***. / Reducing the amount of cheese or using low fat cheese ***[1 mark]*** and adding another topping to add more flavour ***[1 mark]***. / Replacing the flour in the dough ***[1 mark]*** with gluten-free flour ***[1 mark]***. / Replacing the ham ***[1 mark]*** with vegetables or an alternative protein food ***[1 mark]***.

Answers

Page 40 — Standard Food Components — 1

1 a) A ready made ingredient / food component ***[1 mark]***.

b) E.g. any three of: lasagne sheets ***[1 mark]*** / pre-made tomato sauce ***[1 mark]*** / pre-made cheese sauce ***[1 mark]*** / pre-packed meat ***[1 mark]*** / pre-cut vegetables ***[1 mark]***.

2 E.g.

- Pie filling which is prepared elsewhere ***[1 mark]***.
  Advantage: It saves time ***[1 mark]***. / It's more cost-effective to buy in the pie filling ***[1 mark]***. / Food preparation is safer and more hygienic ***[1 mark]***. / Fewer specialist skills are needed by staff ***[1 mark]***. / Less machinery and specialist equipment is needed ***[1 mark]***. / More likely to get a consistent product ***[1 mark]***.
- Pie filling which is bought in tins ***[1 mark]***.
  Advantage: Food lasts for much longer ***[1 mark]***. / Seasonal foods can be used at any time of the year ***[1 mark]***. / It saves time ***[1 mark]***. / It's more cost-effective to buy in the pie filling because they can be bought in bulk ***[1 mark]***. / Food preparation is safer and more hygienic ***[1 mark]***. / Fewer specialist skills are needed by staff ***[1 mark]***. / Less machinery and specialist equipment is needed ***[1 mark]***. / More likely to get a consistent product ***[1 mark]***.
- Ready made pastry ***[1 mark]***.
  Advantage: Pastry can be stored and lasts for much longer ***[1 mark]***. / It saves the company time ***[1 mark]***. / More cost-effective to buy in the pastry ***[1 mark]***. / Fewer specialist skills are needed by staff ***[1 mark]***. / Less machinery and specialist equipment is needed ***[1 mark]***. / More likely to get a consistent product ***[1 mark]***.
  [1 mark for each standard component, up to 2 marks. 1 mark for each different, suitable advantage, up to 2 marks.]

3 a) E.g. using fresh products may give a better flavour ***[1 mark]***.

b) E.g. any three of: the manufacturer can't pick and choose exactly what they want ***[1 mark]***. / Late delivery from the supplier will hold up the production line ***[1 mark]***. / Extra space might be needed to store a bulk buy of standard components ***[1 mark]***. / There's extra packing and transport involved so it might be bad for the environment/be more expensive ***[1 mark]***.

Page 41 — Standard Food Components — 2

4 a) E.g. it saves the manufacturer time because they don't have to prepare the icing and marzipan first ***[1 mark]***. / It saves the manufacturer money because it is more cost-effective to buy the icing and marzipan in bulk ***[1 mark]***. / It makes the product more likely to be consistent because the icing and marzipan used will all be the same colour, texture, etc. ***[1 mark]***. / Less machinery/equipment/staff are needed by the manufacturer because the icing and marzipan are already prepared ***[1 mark]***.
[1 mark for each advantage, up to 3 marks.]

b) E.g. any two of: cake mix ***[1 mark]*** / chocolate butter cream ***[1 mark]*** / tinned fruit slices ***[1 mark]*** / fruit syrup ***[1 mark]*** / glazed cherries ***[1 mark]***.

5 a) E.g. using standard components reduces the sustainability of a product ***[1 mark]*** as it involves using extra packaging ***[1 mark]***, which uses up a lot of resources, e.g. oil for plastic ***[1 mark]***. It involves extra transport ***[1 mark]***, which means more fossil fuels are burnt / more carbon dioxide is released / global warming is contributed to ***[1 mark]***. Using standard components can reduce the cost of a product ***[1 mark]*** as manufacturers can buy ingredients in bulk which is more cost effective ***[1 mark]***.

b) Any two of: use renewable energy ***[1 mark]***. / Use less packaging ***[1 mark]***. / Use recyclable/biodegradable packaging ***[1 mark]***. / Use biofuels ***[1 mark]***. / Reduce food miles ***[1 mark]***. / Buy local produce ***[1 mark]***.

Page 42 — Scale of Production — 1

1 a) i) E.g. cereal / baked beans / coffee / digestive biscuits / crisps ***[1 mark]***.

ii) E.g. birthday cake / wedding cake ***[1 mark]***.

b) Advantage — any one of: the products made are unique / high quality ***[1 mark]***.
Disadvantage — any one of: expensive process / time-consuming / requires experienced/skilled workers ***[1 mark]***.

2 a) Making specific quantities of a product in one go ***[1 mark]***.

b) E.g. the manufacturer only sells the biscuits to local shops so probably doesn't sell enough to make mass production or continuous flow production cost-effective ***[1 mark]***. The manufacturer makes a range of biscuits so needs to change batches every so often, which can be done easily with batch production ***[1 mark]***. One-off production isn't suitable as the manufacturer wouldn't be able to make one biscuit at a time ***[1 mark]***.

c) E.g. it's cheaper / more cost-effective in the long-term / fewer workers are needed ***[1 mark]***.

d) E.g. new machines would have to be bought / some workers would have to be replaced by machines ***[1 mark]***.

Page 43 — Scale of Production — 2

3 a) Computer Aided Design ***[1 mark]***.

b) i) E.g. the company can easily calculate the product's nutritional value/cost to make/portion size/shelf life ***[1 mark]***.

ii) Any one of: e.g. the company can easily change the packaging design on screen / the packaging can be viewed from any angle/in 3D / it's much quicker/more accurate than designing packaging on paper ***[1 mark]***.

4 a) Computer Aided Manufacture ***[1 mark]***.

b) E.g. any three of: CAM is more accurate/reliable because there is less chance of human error ***[1 mark]***. / Production costs are lower in the long term using CAM because fewer staff are needed ***[1 mark]***. / Using CAM is quicker because computers make the production process more efficient ***[1 mark]***. / Products are more consistent using CAM because they're produced exactly the same each time ***[1 mark]***. / CAM allows any changes to the process to be made very easily via a computer ***[1 mark]***. / CAM can be carried out 24 hours a day, so production can continue even when staff aren't present ***[1 mark]***.

Answers

5 CAD examples, e.g. designing the appearance/packaging of the pizza ***[1 mark]***. / Modelling portion sizes ***[1 mark]***. / Calculating the nutritional content/cost/profit/shelf life ***[1 mark]***. / Analysing sensory data ***[1 mark]***. / Presenting information ***[1 mark]***. / Showing the assembly procedures ***[1 mark]***.
[1 mark for each CAD example, up to two marks.]
CAM examples, e.g. monitoring/changing the production process ***[1 mark]***. / Using computer controlled equipment, e.g. electronic scales ***[1 mark]***. / Weighing out ingredients ***[1 mark]***. / Setting oven temperature/cooking time ***[1 mark]***.
[1 mark for each CAM example, up to 2 marks.]

Page 44 — Quality Control — 1

1 a) Checking that standards are being met, in order to produce a high quality product ***[1 mark]***.

b) E.g. any two of: control checks mean the manufacturer can quickly discover and fix any problems, so time and money aren't wasted ***[1 mark]***. /
The manufacturer can produce consistent products/products that won't harm the consumer ***[1 mark]***. /
They make sure the product meets the design criteria ***[1 mark]***.

2 Any two relevant checks ***[2 marks]***. E.g. checks relating to using the same weights/proportions of ingredients ***[1 mark]*** / size of tin to cook loaves ***[1 mark]*** / ingredients used in each batch ***[1 mark]*** / length of time to knead dough ***[1 mark]*** / temperature of ovens ***[1 mark]*** / packaging and storage prior to distribution ***[1 mark]***.

3 a) Physical contamination ***[1 mark]***.
Any two relevant checks ***[2 marks]***. E.g. check staff are wearing gloves ***[1 mark]***. Pies to be checked before being packaged ***[1 mark]***.

b) Biological contamination ***[1 mark]***.
Any two relevant checks ***[2 marks]***. E.g. check the eggs that are used are fresh ***[1 mark]***. / Check ingredients are stored correctly ***[1 mark]***. / Use regular hygiene checks on ingredients/equipment ***[1 mark]***. / Take samples of the end product / use temperature probes to check all quiches are thoroughly cooked all the way through ***[1 mark]***.

Page 45 — Quality Control — 2

4 E.g. any three of: check ingredients are bought from a reliable supplier ***[1 mark]***. / Visually check the condition of the ingredients/packaging ***[1 mark]***. / Check ingredients have been stored at the correct temperature ***[1 mark]***. / Check the use by/sell by/best before dates to make sure the ingredients are fresh ***[1 mark]***. / Check the weights using computers/digital scales ***[1 mark]***. / Check for any physical/biological/chemical contamination ***[1 mark]***.

5 Relevant check after preparing the working area, e.g. check that equipment has been washed / check surfaces have been sterilised ***[1 mark]***.
Relevant check after preparing ingredients, e.g. check the weights/amounts of ingredients are correct / check that ingredients are fresh / check ingredients have been stored correctly ***[1 mark]***.
Relevant check after mixing ingredients, e.g. check the oven is at the correct temperature ready for baking / visually check the mixture is the right consistency ***[1 mark]***.
Relevant check after baking muffins, e.g. use a temperature probe to check muffins are cooked all the way through / visually check the size/shape/colour of muffins ***[1 mark]***.
Relevant check after leaving muffins to cool before packaging, e.g. randomly sample muffins to check the taste / use a temperature probe to check muffins are cooled all the way through ***[1 mark]***.

Page 46 — Food Contamination and Bacteria — 1

1 Any two of: prawns ***[1 mark]*** / mayonnaise ***[1 mark]*** / salad cream ***[1 mark]***.

2 a) Any three of: sickness ***[1 mark]*** / diarrhoea ***[1 mark]*** / stomach cramps ***[1 mark]*** / fever ***[1 mark]***.

b) Heating food to over 72 °C should kill most of the bacteria ***[1 mark]***.

3 a) Transferring bacteria from raw food to other food ***[1 mark]*** via work surfaces, equipment or your hands ***[1 mark]***.

b) Preparation — e.g. keep knives and chopping boards separate from everything else ***[1 mark]***.
Storage — e.g. never put raw meat and cooked meat together ***[1 mark]***.
Handling — e.g. wash hands thoroughly after handling raw meat ***[1 mark]***.

Page 47 — Food Contamination and Bacteria — 2

4 a) Chicken is moist ***[1 mark]*** and high in protein ***[1 mark]***, so bacteria can grow/multiply very quickly ***[1 mark]***.

b) E.g. after the chicken has been cooked it should be served straight away ***[1 mark]***.

c) Purchasing chicken — always buy from a reputable supplier to be sure it's high quality ***[1 mark]***. /
Make sure you'll be able to use the chicken before its use by date ***[1 mark]***. / Check it carefully before buying to make sure it isn't off ***[1 mark]***. / Check the packaging carefully to check it isn't damaged and the seal is intact ***[1 mark]***.
Storing chicken — follow the storage instructions, e.g. store between 0 to 5 °C ***[1 mark]***. / Rotate stock/use old purchases first, before they go out of date ***[1 mark]***. / Keep chicken sealed or covered up ***[1 mark]***. / Keep raw chicken away from other foods ***[1 mark]***.
Cooking chicken — ensure the centre of the chicken is heated to 72 °C ***[1 mark]***. / Cook for the correct amount of time ***[1 mark]***. / Make sure the chicken is cooked all the way through ***[1 mark]***.
[Maximum of 2 marks for each of purchasing chicken, storing chicken and cooking chicken].

Page 48 — Preservation — 1

1 a) 72 °C ***[1 mark]***.

b) E.g. canning / bottling / pasteurisation ***[1 mark]***.

2 a) i) Vinegar is too acidic / changes the pH so bacteria can't grow ***[1 mark]***.

ii) Salt absorbs water from bacteria, making them shrivel up and die ***[1 mark]***.

b) E.g. salted meat/fish ***[1 mark]***.

c) E.g. they can change the taste ***[1 mark]*** and colour ***[1 mark]*** of food.

Answers

3 Because bacteria grow and multiply fastest/very fast within the danger zone ***[1 mark]***, making food potentially unsafe to eat ***[1 mark]***.

Page 49 — Preservation — 2

4 a) i) 0 and 5 °C ***[1 mark]***.

ii) Because chilling slows the growth of bacteria, so food is safer for longer ***[1 mark]***.

b) Advantages — e.g. freezing food greatly extends its shelf life ***[1 mark]***. / Frozen food keeps all its nutrients (unlike heating methods of preservation) ***[1 mark]***. / Freezing food stops bacteria growing/makes bacteria dormant ***[1 mark]***. / Freezing food helps it to keep its colour and flavour ***[1 mark]***.
[1 mark for each advantage, up to 2 marks].
Disadvantages — e.g. freezing food doesn't kill the bacteria ***[1 mark]***. Freezing food can change its texture ***[1 mark]***.
[1 mark for each disadvantage, up to 2 marks].

5 a) The chocolates should be eaten before 01.03.13 ***[1 mark]***. After this date, their quality will decrease ***[1 mark]*** although they'll probably still be safe to eat ***[1 mark]***.

b) The doughnuts have a short shelf life and must be eaten by 01.01.12 ***[1 mark]***. The use by date is given as a safety warning ***[1 mark]*** because the food is high-risk/may be unsafe if eaten after that date ***[1 mark]***.

Page 50 — Domestic and Industrial Equipment — 1

1 a) Steamer / microwave ***[1 mark]***.

b) E.g. vegetables keep more of their taste/colour/texture ***[1 mark]***. / Food doesn't break up because it doesn't have to be drained ***[1 mark]***. / Microwaves are more efficient/less energy is used ***[1 mark]***.

2 a) The temperature of the middle of the food can be checked using a temperature probe ***[1 mark]***.
The middle of high-risk foods must be heated to 72 °C or more to kill bacteria/reduce the risk of food poisoning ***[1 mark]***.

b) E.g. any three of: wash hands before and after using the temperature probe ***[1 mark]***. / Thoroughly clean the probe before and after use ***[1 mark]***. / Always read the instructions carefully before equipment use ***[1 mark]***. / Train workers how to use a temperature probe ***[1 mark]***. / Train workers to follow health and safety regulations ***[1 mark]***. / Regularly test the probe ***[1 mark]***.

3 a) Bread maker/dough hook attachment for a food processor ***[1 mark]***. This will mix the dough consistently/the same every time ***[1 mark]***. /
It saves time/effort of doing it by hand ***[1 mark]***. /
It's more hygienic than doing it by hand ***[1 mark]***.
[1 mark for naming electrical equipment and up to 2 marks for relevant reasons].

b) Blender/food processor ***[1 mark]***. This will mix the ingredients together to get a smooth result ***[1 mark]***. /
It saves time/effort of doing it by hand ***[1 mark]***. /
It gets a consistent product using the same settings ***[1 mark]***.
[1 mark for naming electrical equipment and up to 2 marks for relevant reasons].

Page 51 — Domestic and Industrial Equipment — 2

4 a) E.g. each biscuit is cut to the same size so will cook the same/fit into the packaging/portions are controlled ***[1 mark]***. Biscuits are the same shape so have the same appearance/human error is reduced ***[1 mark]***.

b) E.g. products are cooked for a precise length of time so they'll be the same every time ***[1 mark]***. Products are cooked at the same temperature so they'll be the same every time ***[1 mark]***.

5 E.g. computerised weighing equipment is quicker and easier to use than weighing things non-electrically, e.g. using a balance pan ***[1 mark]***. Products are consistent ***[1 mark]*** because they can be accurately weighed with less room for human error, e.g. to within 0.05 g ***[1 mark]***. Scales can be preset to weigh different ingredients, which saves time ***[1 mark]***.

Section Four — Marketing and Environment

Page 52 — Social Issues — 1

1 Fruit salad — e.g. people trying to lose weight ***[1 mark]*** as they need to eat low-fat foods ***[1 mark]***. / Elderly people ***[1 mark]*** as they may need to cut down on fats in their diet ***[1 mark]***. / People concerned with healthy eating ***[1 mark]*** as it will contain some of their five a day ***[1 mark]***.
High energy snack bar — e.g. athletes ***[1 mark]*** as they need food that provides lots of energy ***[1 mark]***. / People with active jobs ***[1 mark]*** as they need food that provides lots of energy ***[1 mark]***.
Calcium enriched cereal — e.g. pregnant women ***[1 mark]*** as they need extra calcium for healthy baby development ***[1 mark]***. / Toddlers/children ***[1 mark]*** as they need calcium for growth and development ***[1 mark]***.

2 a) i) In some religions certain foods are banned / foods must be prepared in a particular way ***[1 mark]***.

ii) Religion — e.g. Islam ***[1 mark]***.
Design feature — e.g. the curry dishes shouldn't contain any pork as this is banned in Islam ***[1 mark]***.
Food should be prepared so that it is Halal ***[1 mark]***.

b) E.g. how convenient the product is ***[1 mark]***. / The age of the target market ***[1 mark]***. / The ethical issues involved in producing the product, e.g. animal welfare/environmental impact of packaging ***[1 mark]***.

Page 53 — Social Issues — 2

3 Sketch should show:

- Suitable snack product for children, e.g. a small product that can be eaten quickly ***[1 mark]***.
- Clear notes explaining why the appearance would appeal to children, e.g. colourful, fun ***[1 mark]***.
- Clear notes explaining why the ingredients would appeal to children, e.g. sweet tasting ***[1 mark]***.
- Clear notes explaining how the economic needs of children have been accounted for in the design, e.g. cheap for children to purchase ***[1 mark]***.

Answers

E.g. a chocolate bar:

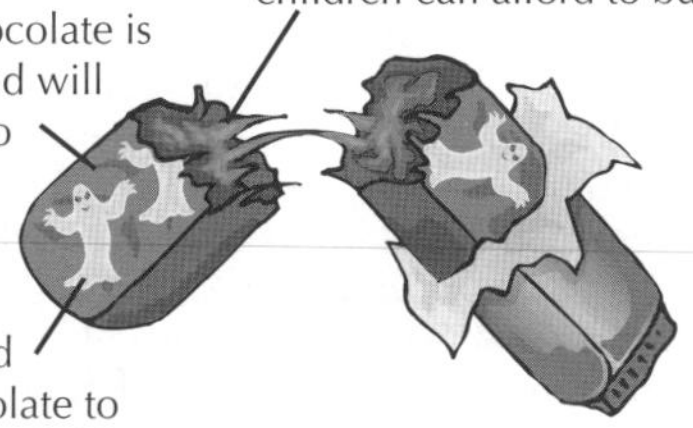

4 a) E.g. the percentage sales of exotic fruits/mangoes/ pineapples/coconuts has increased between 1970 and 2000 ***[1 mark]***. The percentage sales of apples/pears has decreased between 1970 and 2000 ***[1 mark]***.

b) E.g. any two of: more people are aware of exotic fruits ***[1 mark]***. / Better transport means exotic fruits are more easily available ***[1 mark]***. / Society has become more multicultural so a greater variety of fruit is available for people to try ***[1 mark]***.

Page 54 — Environmental Issues — 1

1 a) i) A process or material that can be used without causing permanent damage to the environment or using up finite resources ***[1 mark]***.

ii) E.g. any two of: it contains bluefin tuna which is in short supply ***[1 mark]***. / Energy is used to process the food/make the packaging, using up resources like oil and gas ***[1 mark]***. / Trees are used up to make the cardboard packaging ***[1 mark]***. / Oil is used up to make the plastic packaging ***[1 mark]***. / A mixture of plastic and cardboard packaging can be difficult to recycle ***[1 mark]***.

b) i) The distance food travels from where it's produced to where it's sold ***[1 mark]***.

ii) E.g. it lowers the cost of transporting the food ***[1 mark]***.

c) E.g. any two of: reducing the amount of packaging ***[1 mark]***. / Only using packaging that is made from renewable resources, e.g. cardboard ***[1 mark]***. / Only using packaging materials that can easily be recycled, e.g. cardboard ***[1 mark]***. / Avoiding scarce resources ***[1 mark]***.

2 a) E.g. any two of: food may be labelled as free range, so the consumer knows the animal was free to roam ***[1 mark]***. / Food may be labelled as organic, so the consumer knows the animal welfare standards were high/the animals weren't given growth hormones ***[1 mark]***. / Food may be labelled with the Red Tractor symbol, so the consumer knows that animal welfare standards met those set down by the Assured Food Standards scheme ***[1 mark]***.

b) E.g. any two of: it means that the farmers and workers in the developing world who produced the food received a fair price for the food ***[1 mark]***. / The producers of the food had decent working conditions ***[1 mark]***. / The food was produced in reputable, registered farms ***[1 mark]***. / Profits from the sale of the food are used for local, community projects ***[1 mark]***.

Page 55 — Environmental Issues — 2

3 a) i) E.g. the amount of organic vegetables consumed has increased ***[1 mark]***. / The amount of non-organic vegetables consumed has decreased ***[1 mark]***. / A larger proportion of the vegetables consumed in Byrnshire were organic in 2005 than in 1980 ***[2 marks]***. ***[Up to 2 marks available for description.]***
Reasons: e.g. more consumers cared about the environmental impacts of food production in 2005 than in 1980 ***[1 mark]***. / More people were aware of organic farming in 2005 than in 1980 ***[1 mark]***. / Organic foods were more widely available in 2005 ***[1 mark]***. / More people could afford to buy organic foods in 2005 ***[1 mark]***. / Organic foods were more fashionable in 2005 ***[1 mark]***. ***[1 mark for each sensible reason, up to 2 marks.]***

b) i) Organic farming isn't as efficient and so less food is produced per acre ***[1 mark]***.

ii) Organic food is more expensive ***[1 mark]***.

4 Advantages — e.g. using local food reduces transport costs ***[1 mark]***. / It reduces the amount of pollution caused by transporting food ***[1 mark]***. / It reduces the amount of resources used up to transport the food ***[1 mark]***.
[1 mark for each advantage, up to 2 marks].
Disadvantages — e.g. certain foods won't be available all year round ***[1 mark]***. / Some foods won't be available at all because they can't be grown locally ***[1 mark]***.
[1 mark for each disadvantage, up to 2 marks].

Page 56 — Labelling — 1

1 a) 33.0 g ***[1 mark]***.

b) This isn't a reasonable claim ***[1 mark]*** because the nutritional information shows that the snack contains 33.0 g of fat per 100 g / the snack is nearly a third fat ***[1 mark]***.

2 a) The product is suitable for vegetarians/meat free ***[1 mark]***.
E.g. it helps people who do not eat animal products because of personal/religious beliefs to know if the food is suitable for them ***[1 mark]***. It helps people who are allergic to animal products to know if the food is safe for them to eat ***[1 mark]***.

b) The product may contain nuts ***[1 mark]***.
E.g. any two of: it lets people who are allergic to nuts know that the product may not be safe for them to eat ***[1 mark]***. / It lets consumers know that the product has been made in an area where there are nuts, so it could be contaminated ***[1 mark]***. / It lets consumers know that nuts or nut traces may be in the product even if they're not listed in the ingredients ***[1 mark]***.

c) Some or all of the packaging can be recycled ***[1 mark]***.
E.g. it reminds consumers to recycle the packaging ***[1 mark]***. It helps consumers to dispose of the packaging in a suitable way ***[1 mark]***.

Page 57 — Labelling — 2

3 a) i) Foods that are high risk need to have a use by date. ***[1 mark]***. Non high risk foods only need a best before date ***[1 mark]***.

ii) Use by date — e.g. meat / fish / milk ***[1 mark]***.
Best before date — e.g. bread / cereal / tinned food ***[1 mark]***.

Answers

b) Sketch should show:

- Appropriate design of label with all information shown clearly ***[1 mark]***.
- Use by date ***[1 mark]***.
- Name of product ***[1 mark]***.
- Weight ***[1 mark]***.
- Name and address of manufacturer ***[1 mark]***.
- Cooking instructions ***[1 mark]***.
- Ingredients and annotation explaining the order ingredients should be listed in ***[1 mark]***.
- Storage instructions ***[1 mark]***.

E.g:

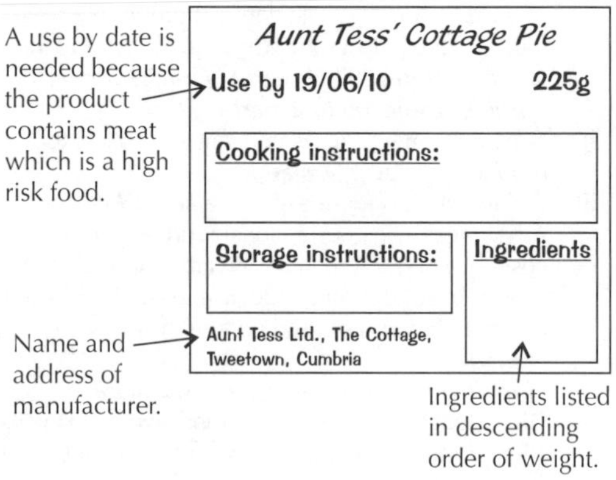

Page 58 — Packaging — 1

1 E.g. any three of: to keep the product together ***[1 mark]***. / To protect the product from being damaged whilst it's being transported/displayed/stored ***[1 mark]***. / To preserve the product ***[1 mark]***. / To avoid contamination ***[1 mark]***. / To identify what the product is ***[1 mark]***. / To give customers useful information ***[1 mark]***.

2 a) i) Cardboard ***[1 mark]***.

ii) Advantages — e.g. lightweight ***[1 mark]***. / Flexible ***[1 mark]***. / Easy to print on ***[1 mark]***. / Biodegradable ***[1 mark]***. / Easy/cheap to recycle ***[1 mark]***.
[1 mark for each advantage, up to 2 marks].
Disadvantages — e.g. you can't see the contents ***[1 mark]***. / It's not very rigid so could get squashed ***[1 mark]***.
[1 mark for each disadvantage, up to 2 marks].

b) Plastic ***[1 mark]***.

c) E.g. Both cardboard and plastic can be recycled ***[1 mark]***. Cardboard is biodegradable but plastic is not ***[1 mark]***. Cardboard is made using a renewable resource (trees) whilst plastic comes from a non-renewable resource (oil) ***[1 mark]***. So cardboard is a more sustainable material than plastic ***[1 mark]***.

Page 59 — Packaging — 2

3 a) E.g. any two of:
Product: cheese. Packaging: e.g. vacuum packaging ***[1 mark]***. Vacuum packing involves putting the food into plastic packaging and then sucking the air out so that the food is kept in oxygen free conditions ***[1 mark]***. / Modified atmosphere packaging ***[1 mark]***. The food is put into plastic with a mixture of oxygen, nitrogen and carbon dioxide in particular proportions and is then sealed and chilled ***[1 mark]***.
Product: meat. Packaging: e.g. vacuum packaging ***[1 mark]***. Vacuum packing involves putting the food into plastic packaging and then sucking the air out so that the food is kept in oxygen free conditions ***[1 mark]***. / Modified atmosphere packaging ***[1 mark]***. The food is put into plastic with a mixture of oxygen, nitrogen and carbon dioxide in particular proportions and is then sealed and chilled ***[1 mark]***.
Product: crisps. Packaging: e.g. modified atmosphere packaging ***[1 mark]***. The food is put into plastic with a mixture of oxygen, nitrogen and carbon dioxide in particular proportions and is then sealed and chilled ***[1 mark]***. ***[Up to 2 marks for different descriptions of the types of packaging]***.

b) i) Nanotechnology is a new technology that involves using very small particles to improve the qualities of a product ***[1 mark]***.

ii) E.g. any two of: to improve the packaging's ability to keep out moisture/oxygen ***[1 mark]***. / To make the packaging change colour to show when the product has gone off ***[1 mark]***. / To make the packaging stronger ***[1 mark]***. / To make the packaging heat-resistant ***[1 mark]***. / Nanoparticles could be added to kill microorganisms and keep the food fresher ***[1 mark]***.
[Answer applies to any of the products chosen].

iii) It would make it more expensive ***[1 mark]***.

Page 60 — Packaging — 3

4
- Design shows a suitable container for pasta sauce, e.g. airtight, clearly labelled ***[1 mark]***.
- Design shows packaging to be made from more sustainable materials than the initial design, e.g. glass container, paper label ***[1 mark]***.
- Clear notes explaining why the design is more sustainable than the initial design ***[1 mark for each sensible annotation, up to 3 marks]***.

E.g:

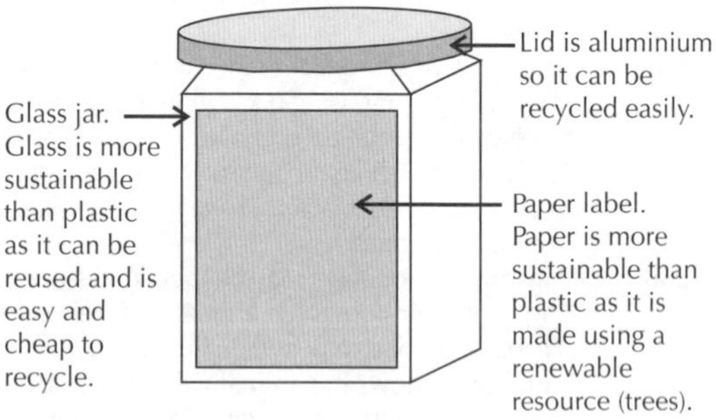

ISBN 978 1 84762 403 1

9 781847 624031

TFAA41